Integrating Literacy Naturally

Integrating Literacy Naturally

Avoiding the One-Size-Fits-All Curriculum in Early Childhood

Kim Pinkerton and Amelia Hewitt

ROWMAN & LITTLEFIELD
Lanham • Boulder • New York • London

Published by Rowman & Littlefield
An imprint of The Rowman & Littlefield Publishing Group, Inc.
4501 Forbes Boulevard, Suite 200, Lanham, Maryland 20706
www.rowman.com

6 Tinworth Street, London SE11 5AL, United Kingdom

Copyright © 2020 by Kim Pinkerton & Amelia Hewitt

All rights reserved. No part of this book may be reproduced in any form or by any electronic or mechanical means, including information storage and retrieval systems, without written permission from the publisher, except by a reviewer who may quote passages in a review.

British Library Cataloguing in Publication Information Available

Library of Congress Cataloging-in-Publication Data
Names: Pinkerton, Kim, 1973- author. |
    Hewitt, Amelia, 1966- author.
Title: Integrating literacy naturally : avoiding the one-size-fits-all
    curriculum in early childhood / Kim Pinkerton and Amelia Hewitt.
Description: Lanham : Rowman & Littlefield, [2020] |
    Includes bibliographical references and index.
Identifiers: LCCN 2020001547 (print) | LCCN 2020001548 (ebook) |
    ISBN 9781475853889 (cloth) | ISBN 9781475853896 (paperback) |
    ISBN 9781475853902 (ebook)
Subjects: LCSH: Language arts (Early childhood) |
    Literacy. | Early childhood education—Curricula. |
    Individualized education programs. | Reflective teaching. |
    Teaching—Methodology.
Classification: LCC LB1139.5.L35 P56 2020 (print) |
    LCC LB1139.5.L35 (ebook) | DDC 372.6—dc23
LC record available at https://lccn.loc.gov/2020001547
LC ebook record available at https://lccn.loc.gov/2020001548

Contents

Foreword: Literacy as a Human Activity		vii
Preface		xi
Acknowledgments		xiii
Introduction		xv
Principle 1:	Love Literacy	1
Principle 2:	Build a Library of Books	19
Principle 3:	Avoid the One-Size-Fits-All Approach	37
Principle 4:	Link Development and Play to Literacy Learning	53
Principle 5:	Share Daily, Delightful Read Alouds	69
Principle 6:	Use Children's Texts to Teach Content	89
Principle 7:	Cultivate Literacy Skills with Balanced Instruction	107
Principle 8:	Connect Literacy Learning with a Reimagined Literacy Workshop	131
Appendix A: Children's Texts List		145
Appendix B: Resources List		151

References	155
Teacher Spotlight Biographies	165
Index	169
Author Biographies	177

Foreword

Literacy as a Human Activity

Mohja Kahf, Syrian-born, American poet from the University of Arkansas, writes a blessing for the future in "Fayetteville as in Fate" from her collection of poems *E-mails from Scheherazad* (2006):

May their children e-mail one another and not bomb one another
May they download each other's mother's bread recipes
May they sell yams and yogurts to each other at a conscionable profit
May they learn each other's tongue and put words into each other's mouths
Say *Amen*
Say آمين
Say it, say it.[1]

As a lifelong advocate for preparing and strengthening educators of young children, I seek books that advocate for effective practices that promote social justice and equity for all children. *Integrating Literacy Naturally* is a great addition to my list. The book's focus, developing young children's literacy practices, is on the forefront of the minds of many early childhood educators, school and childcare administrators, as well as families.

These stakeholders often address particular skills such as writing names and identifying the alphabet before children enter kindergarten, and by first grade continuing to develop their literacy skills on a linear projection via decoding, comprehending, and reading books at an assigned level. It almost seems like a race, instead of children learning according to their "unique inner clocks" (Genishi & Dyson, 2009, p. 37). And during the race, many children fall behind by not achieving particular skills and feeling defeated with little, if any, confidence in their abilities.

Authors Kim Pinkerton and Amelia Hewitt argue that literacy skills are important, but what is more important is that children are active literacy learners and that they develop a passion for reading. A passion for reading involves children losing themselves in a book they are reading, imagining their own lives in different spaces, and thinking about the characters and the characters' next moves in the story, and, as Kahf's quote represents, sharing their lives with other human beings.

Following are four interrelated contributions to developing children's passion for reading that I found extremely interesting in this unique book:

- Allowing teachers to make decisions that promote a passion for literacy
- Knowing children as individuals
- Using read alouds often
- Assessing informally

First, the competence of educators is highlighted when it comes to developing children's literacy lives. This perspective seems to have been lost within the initiatives of prescriptive curriculum, standards, high-stakes testing, and expecting students to exhibit specific skills and behaviors within the walls of the school environment.

Second, by describing this book as a guide and not a manual, Pinkerton and Hewitt bring educators back to their original intentions for entering the teaching profession. One intention was to have an impact on children's learning by knowing them as individuals with unique strengths, rhythms, abilities, and ways of "reading" and expressing knowledge about the world.

Because each child pursues a passion for learning differently, the teacher and child create a relationship where the teacher recognizes and plans for the child's passions. In other words, teachers respect children more than a number on a test through their caring about and nurturing of each child's literacy journey. They perceive children as inquisitive human beings who want to connect and belong to their worlds, that is, their families, peers, educators, and other community members. It's this type of curiosity that inspires children's learning.

Third, this type of curiosity is promoted through the instructional event of read alouds that the authors discuss for promoting each child's literacy journey. The authors caution educators to not use read alouds solely for teaching literacy skills but also for helping students find enjoyable, engaging, and favorite books selected according to children's interests. These read alouds help young children see their world. Sims-Bishop (1990) writes about the value of books where "literature transforms human experience and reflects it back to us, and in that reflection we can see our own lives and experiences as part of the larger human experience. Reading, then, becomes a means of self-affirmation, and readers often seek their mirrors in books" (p. ix).

Fourth, I found the authors' content regarding educators' use of ongoing informal assessments (e.g., documentation through educators' written notes, photographs, children's products, video/audio recordings) of their children's literacy practices invaluable. Teachers often feel rushed to get through specific material and reach some type of artificial goal of students' learning of the material through a standardized assessment in the form of a quiz, end-of-the-unit test, and so on. These types of assessments are problematic because often young children are unable to express their knowledge through this format. Furthermore, these assessments are designed to only show what children don't know, which can be frustrating for parents, children, and educators. Parents can't figure out how to help their children learn the information, educators know children have more knowledge than what the test score represents, and children only receive general messages that they need to "do better."

Authentic, informal assessments embedded during parts of lessons, units, and other activities, like the ones highlighted by Pinkerton and Hewitt, provide educators opportunities to assist in accessing student learning. Knowing what children are and are not learning assists educators in knowing how to revise their lessons, whether it's clarifying the instructions, changing the pace, or spending more time on the content. This type of assessing leads to more impactful learning experiences.

Teachers who have internalized these four key contributions featured in Pinkerton and Hewitt's book have a greater opportunity of fostering lifelong reading from a young age. The goal is for young children to ultimately have a similar experience either to the one that Naomi Shihab Nye (2008) writes about in her poem "Before I Read *The Kite Runner*" or to the one that I had when I was getting ready to fly back from Brazil to the United States.

I had boarded the plane and was getting ready to read *The Day the World Came to Town: 9/11 in Gander, Newfoundland* by Jim Defede. I had the book on my lap when a man from Australia going to his seat stopped and commented, "What a great book." A woman from the United Kingdom who sat across the aisle said to me, "I remember where I was on that day." Another person sitting next to me remarked, "This book gave me hope that humanity does indeed have the capacity to care for each other." And, the flight attendant walking down the aisle looked at the book and gasped, "So powerful."

The fact that I had a parallel experience to what Naomi Shihab Nye describes in her poem shows the absolute power that books have. My wish is that when children become adults, teachers will have instilled in them a passion for reading where they make human connections, like these people on the plane did. This text is the guide that can help teachers to be that inspiration for young readers and writers.

Laurie Katz,
Professor of Early Childhood Education at
the Ohio State University

NOTE

1 "*Fayetteville as in Fate*," by Mohja Kahf in *E-mails from Scheherazad*, by Mohja Kahf. Gainesville: University Press of Florida, 2003, lines 53–59 on pp. 7.

REFERENCES

Genishi, C., & Dyson, A. H. (2009). *Children, Language, and Literacy: Diverse Learners in Diverse Times*. New York: Teachers College Press.

Kahf, M. (2006). *E-mails from Scheherazad*. Gainesville, FL: University Press of Florida.

Nye, N.S. (2008). *Honeybee*. NY, NY: Greenwillow Books.

Sims Bishop, R. (1990). Mirrors, windows, and sliding glass doors. In Hughes Moir, Melissa Cain, & Leslie Prosak-Beres (Eds.) *Collected Perspectives: Choosing and Using Books for the Classroom*, 6(3), Boston: Christopher-Gordon Publishers.

Preface

Dear Reader,

This book is a work of heart. Our hearts hurt when we see classrooms where literacy is being broken down into worksheets, there is no joy in reading, no one is individualizing literacy instruction, books are absent, and playful learning is nonexistent. Even our very own preservice teachers who we train sometimes become immobilized by the structured routine of high-stakes literacy instruction. Our hearts weep for the children who may never learn to love literacy the way that we do.

Because our hearts grow heavy when any child says, "I hate to read," we decided it was time to lend our voices to the conversations about literacy and provide teachers with tools for building up children and facilitating literacy learning for all. We wanted to share our passion for literacy and show how books and children can be the forefront of teaching.

We found teachers who share our passion and our philosophy for teaching literacy and were willing to share their voices with you too. They confirm that children are the center of literacy teaching. These teachers grow young minds and help children feel secure in their literacy knowledge and experiences. In their classrooms, they hear comments daily like "I did it!" and "That was so cool!" These teachers get children excited about being a part of the literacy learning process.

Along with us, these spotlight teachers believe that literacy is the key to building a world with infinite possibilities. Literacy *is* the foundation for all learning. It is the most natural way to integrate all content. In essence, literacy is at the heart of life.

We want to make literacy usable, meaningful, and lovable for you and the young children with whom you work. We want our passion for growing lovers of literacy to be transferred to you. With this book, we hope that you:

- Become knowledgeable about teaching literacy
- See the importance of knowing the children you are teaching
- Learn to engage children with authentic texts
- Encourage exploration and interaction with literacy materials in playful ways
- Urge curiosity and questioning along the way

When you close this book, we want literacy to become part of your heart so much so that you will not be able to live without it!
Happy reading,
Kim and Amelia

Acknowledgments

We are so grateful to everyone who helped us grow as readers and writers along life's journey. There are so many who we could each mention: professional colleagues, literacy and early childhood organizations, our preservice teachers, authors of trade books, friends, classroom teachers, and more. A big, collective hug goes out to you all. But, we can name those who had a more direct hand in the writing of this book. Brian, Cade, and Kendall, thank you for being Kim's supportive family who always told her that she could and didn't roll too many eyes when she refused to get up from the computer. A great big Thank You to Amelia's family: Joey, Haley, and Hunter. Thank you for supporting her through all the hours spent on Zoom, reading chapters in the car, or time spent working on edits while on vacation. This book is a part of all of us, and we could not have done it without all of you! To Laurie, Christina, Susan, Carolyn, Joceylyn, and Laura, thank you for the beautifully supportive words and comments about the book. We are forever indebted to you and will always try to model your kindness and thoughtfulness. To Gabe, Anna, Kelsey, Joni, Maria, Isabel, Ghida, Courtney, Brandy, Shannon, and Kecia, thank you for all that you do to grow lifelong lovers of literacy. Keep lighting that torch for others. A shout out to Parker for being our artist. Finally, thanks to the NCTE team who assisted Laurie in revising the position statement entitled "The Act of Reading: Instructional Foundations and Policy Guidelines," which ultimately led to their guidance in the compilation of the foreword for this book. Curt Dudley-Marling, Ashlee Meredith, Diane Miller, and Joseph Pizzo provided inspiration for the words. Thanks also to Melissa Wilson who provided a close read of the foreword and invaluable input. This whole book was certainly shaped by many.

Introduction

Why literacy? Literacy is just so much bigger now than it ever has been. Simply being able to read the classics (or SparkNotes for so many children) and write essays is not enough to be fully literate. Readers and writers need adept receptive (listening) and expressive (speaking) language. They need decoding, encoding, and meaning-based skills. They need to navigate and expertly use the digital world, where unique literacy abilities are a must.

While the U.S. Constitution does not guarantee it, some have said that literacy is a civil right. Without it, adults have difficulty navigating the professional world, and doors that could have been opened by an ability to read and write are closed. That grand pursuit of life, liberty, and happiness is often thwarted for the illiterate. Being literate is an essential life skill. *Literacy* is that important!

Why young children? The early years of literacy development are critical to later reading success. Master literacy teachers are the key to ensuring that young children acquire what they need to navigate the complex world of literacy. We just cannot afford to botch literacy teaching in these early grades. So much depends on you, as an early literacy teacher. Because of that, young children need you to be skilled and passionate about literacy so that you can help them acquire both the old and new literacies on their pursuit of life, liberty, and happiness. *You* are that important!

Why this book? Our book is designed with a love of literacy in mind. It is not a manual, but it is a guide for how to coach literacy learning in the early years. In fact, if you glance at the table of contents, you can clearly see the path that we will take on this journey together. We feel passionate about you loving literacy and children and knowing that time in authentic interactions with reading and writing will give you the best chance to avoid one-sized literacy instruction. We want to gently lead you to new understandings about how this can work for your literacy teaching with the most fragile readers and writers. *This book* is that important!

However, as we mentioned, this book is not a manual, so when you open the book, don't expect to see steps for teaching literacy. Instead, prepare for discussions about meeting the individual literacy needs of children in developmentally appropriate ways. We want to be your guide as you discover that teaching literacy is so much more than drill about skills. This book serves as a model for how children's texts can take the lead when young readers and writers learn strategies and skills in the early years. It is an anthology of important principles early childhood teachers can use to make literacy learning both playful and intentional.

So, why are we giving you the guide, instead of the manual? First, there is no magic potion for growing expert readers and writers. If there were, this book would not be needed. However, if we were going to point to something close to a magical ingredient, that ingredient would be children's texts and the fact that young readers and writers need time in those texts. They need to read and write.

Think about this. What if a high school basketball coach has twenty practices before the first, big game? In each practice, the players do drills for dribbling, shooting, and passing. They get really good at standing in front of a partner and passing the ball. They wait patiently in line to shoot the ball. And, they can even walk deftly up and down the court dribbling the ball without missing a beat.

Then, they show up for their first game against a neighboring high school. The coach says, "Put what you learned from your drills together and get out there and play." Yet, they have never played a basketball game before that point! What would happen in that game? It would be chaos. The drills haven't been connected together into plays or strategy.

The point is that no coach in her right mind would ever spend every practice just doing drills. Yes, there might be some isolated drills, but most of the practice would be devoted to playing basketball while the coach continues to teach based on what the players are doing in the moment of the game.

It is the same for reading and writing. Some isolated skill teaching is needed, but most of the time, children should be reading and writing. They can be doing that with children's texts as their model. Time in a text far outweighs isolated practice. So, with this book,

- We will guide you.
- We will encourage you to grow as a reader and writer.
- We will share ideas for scaffolding playful literacy learning while children are actually in a text.
- We will suggest lots of children's text titles, more than 100 in fact.

- We will inform your understanding about best practices for reading and writing to and with young children.
- We will encourage you to avoid one-size-fits-all literacy teaching.
- And, we will challenge you to stretch your thinking about thematic literacy learning.

If you are ready to change the way young children are taught literacy, read on. Our book was written in a way that allows you to take action based on your teaching needs. It is a book of principles to inspire you in your work with children in literacy every day. Since it is so important to integrate literacy naturally, we designed an action item list of sorts with the Table of Contents (and within the headings inside of each principle), but we are leaving it up to you to decide how those actions would work with your teaching and your young readers and writer. We welcome you to use this book as a guide to nurture your own love of literacy and cultivate enthusiasm for literacy learning in children. Let this book be your guide as you become a master early literacy teacher.

Principle 1

Love Literacy

Loving literacy is the primary principle, no question. That is why we are starting this book right here. Why is it so important for teachers of young children to love literacy? The answer is simple. You must be a reader and writer in order to effectively grow young readers and writers. This principle is going to help you see why that is so and hopefully inspire you to cultivate your reading and writing habits, whether you are just planting your own literacy seed or you have literacy roots that are firmly established.

Like some adults, young children sometimes struggle to have a good relationship with reading and writing. Think about this. As infants, oral language is the first element of literacy acquired. It seems to come pretty easily to most people, and we rarely have to teach someone to enjoy communicating with other human beings. Reading and writing, on the other hand, often end up as pariahs. So, in order to learn to love all parts of literacy, we need to do a little work to love reading and writing (Bear, Invernizzi, Templeton, & Johnston, 2016).

In principle 1, you will learn more about what it really means to love reading and writing, why it is important for teachers to love both, and how to develop and nurture that love.

TALK ABOUT READING AND WRITING

Find Out What Readers Do

Very rarely do two book-loving literacy teachers get together and not talk about books. They make enthusiastic book recommendations, talk about

Diane: I'm so busy! I just want to find some time to sit down and read a book. Maybe I won't take my computer on my trip so that I can just read the books that I've downloaded to my iPad. I downloaded *Heartless*, the one you told me about.

Margaret: Yeah, I did that when I went on my trip, and I read *Nemisis* and *Genesis*. I didn't even take my computer or get Internet access. It was great! Now, I want to read *Crazy Rich Asians*.

Diane: Oh yeah! We should both read that and then see the movie!

Margaret: Yes, let's do it! You know what else you should read? Ruth Ware has a book called, *The Woman in Cabin 10*. It is sort of like the Gillian Flynn books that we've read but not quite as crazy. Oh, I heard they made a movie about *Sharp Objects*.

Diane: Eww, that's the one where she is the cutter! It's the one with the pigs. That scene is burned on my brain.

Figure 1.1 A little talk about reading

experiences reading, share their love of characters, and much more. These conversations exemplify a love of reading. In figure 1.1, you will read about two teachers, Diane and Margaret. They are having a conversation about their reading experiences.

Teachers who love to read have a fever for books, and their conversations about books are contagious. People who talk with them want to read what they read and want to feel the excitement of living in a story; this carries into their conversations about books that children read as well.

Uncover How Writers Think

People who love to write use it daily. They are creative and have been likened to artists by scholars like Lucy Calkins (1994). For them writing is a process, often a slow process. It takes thoughtfulness and time as it evolves. Most writers don't begin by writing an epic novel. They have to start with seeds.

Listen to Diane and Margaret, in figure 1.2, as they grapple with this concept about writing. Think about where you fit into the conversation.

People who love to write do not limit themselves with boundaries about what writing is. They enjoy the process of moving from the seed to create pieces that grow over time. They consider themselves writers at every phase.

Diane has not defined herself as a writer because she does not yet have confidence about the process. Those who do have that confidence exude it.

Diane: I'm not a writer. I only write for work, more academically.

Margaret: What? You write all of the time. You have lots of notes about teaching, activities that you want to try, and books that you want to buy.

Diane: Well, those are just notes.

Margaret: What about your notebook and electronic notes that you kept when you were diagnosed with leukemia?

Diane: But, most of what's in there is just lab work and questions for the doctor.

Margaret: That's still writing, and it's a place to find seeds for writing more. What if you went back to your first day of notes and read them? What would you find?

Diane: I would remember that day, how I was feeling, and worries that I had.

Margaret: That's what a writer would do. She would find a seed to expand. The story evolves from those little notes; you just have to take the next step and write your story.

Figure 1.2 A little talk about writing

Despite what Diane might think, she can learn to love writing. She just has to believe in herself and awaken that love for writing.

Where do you stand in your relationship with reading and writing? Do you feel that you are stronger in one area over the other? Think about these questions as you explore how to build a love for reading and writing. Determine how to saturate your life with reading and writing so that a strong foundation for literacy will grow.

BUILD A LOVE FOR READING AND WRITING

Investigate Your Reading Life

What does it mean to love reading? When we really love a book, we get lost in the story, connect with characters, and live vicariously through them, essentially becoming participant observers inside the world of the book. We want others to share in our passion about the book, so we talk obsessively with anyone who will listen. We read and talk voraciously about the book because we are actively seeking another book that will evoke that experience again. It is behavior like this that leads us to think that we really do love reading!

Children who do not love books in this way are destined to be aliterate (can read but choose not to read) in school and as adults. "We have 100 percent interest [in reading] in kindergarten but lose three-quarters of our potential lifetime readers by the time they're eighteen" (Trelease, 2013, p. 1). Adult reading habits are bleak as well, with over half of American adults being aliterate (Trelease, 2013).

These statistics are disheartening and should prompt those of us who teach literacy to want to do more, to be better. It should motivate us to change these statistics. There are so many important reasons why we should feel this way, because when children fail to "develop a mature appreciation of the rewards of reading," they are "thrown off course on the journey to skilled reading" (Snow, Burns, & Griffin, 1998, pp. 4–5). A failure to love reading truly does impact the rest of their lives.

The good news is that if you are reading this book, then you have an interest in working with readers from the beginning. That means *you* are crucial to building a love for lifelong reading. You can begin instilling this foundation from the moment you start teaching young children, but there are a few things that you need to do first: know a lot about the books that your children will want to read and then *read, read, read* books—all kinds of them.

In order to provide these essential literacy components to young children, you must be a reader first. Don't worry. If you have not found your own love for reading yet, we will help you. The journey for the love of books and reading can follow different paths but will end up in the same place: teachers who are readers.

What are your first experiences with books? What kinds of memories do you have? Think about the questions below as you remember.

- Did your journey start with a reading life that wasn't much at all, or have you always been surrounded by reading experiences?
- Did you have enough money to buy new books, or were the only books that you had from yard sales?
- Did your parents take you to visit a public library, did a book mobile visit your community, or did you not get to go to the library until you could drive yourself?
- When you were a child, did you have a teacher who made the reading experience encouraging and exhibited a passion for reading, or were you an adult before you developed a passion for reading?
- When books were around you, did you feel invigorated? Did you love turning the pages and the smell of the books, or did you see books as intimidating?

We ask you these questions to show you that the journey to becoming a voracious reader who owns a robust library does not always have to start with a solid early literacy life. Maybe your first experiences with books were substantial and you want to grow your current reading life, or maybe you have no experiences at all. Never fear. It is never too late to begin or grow your love for reading and for books!

Now that you have considered your early reading experiences, it is time to think about how influential you will be in the early literacy lives of the young children with whom you work. Teachers of literacy have to be readers themselves in order to impact the literacy lives of their children. Why?

- When a child comes to ask you what book to choose next, *you have to know children's literature.*
- When you want to build your classroom library, *you have to know children's literature.*
- When you are trying to match books to a child's interest, *you have to know children's literature.*
- When parents ask you what to read at home, *you have to know children's literature.*

In order for children to develop a lifelong love of reading and books, they need you to have an infectious love of reading. Take a few minutes to answer these questions.

- What are you reading now?
- What books are you sharing with others?
- What books can you not wait to read aloud and add to your classroom library?

Children need teachers who are good reading models, so if you do not feel confident with your answers to the questions, don't be discouraged. Remember what we said earlier; it is never too late to become an avid reader. Here is a little tip to get you started.

⚠ Avoid hiding from reading.

Try:

- Finding a reading model who can make book recommendations for you.
- Visiting your local bookstore and asking employees to help you find a really great book.
- Going to your local library and spending an hour looking at picture books, making note of the authors and illustrators.

Make a habit of doing these three things, or find other activities that will enrich your reading life. And, don't forget to document parts of your journey: authors, titles, and what you discover about the texts. What you read will play a part in how you learn to love writing as well.

Consider Your Writing Life

The journey to love writing is similar to learning to love reading. It requires a parallel commitment. When you begin your writing journey, you have to understand why being a writer is important for teachers of writing; then, you have to evaluate your own history and learn how to grow your writing life.

It seems intuitive that in order to teach writing, you need to be a writer yourself. Being a writer requires that you understand the complexity of the writing process, the struggles that writers have, and the joy of writing. Lucy Calkins (1994) puts it like this. "People who write regularly live with a sense of 'I am one who writes,' and this consciousness engenders an extra-susceptibility, an extra-awareness" (p. 23). Writers do not view writing as a mundane task but a delightful one. And, they learn a lot from their writing experiences. Do you remember the last time a writing experience brought you joy or taught you something about your writing?

If writing is hard for you, it may be difficult to think of a joyous writing occasion. What is it that a writer does that makes it enjoyable? Writers are passionate about words and how those words convey meaning. Writers find pleasure when they create structure, break rules, or find other ways to mold writing to make it their own. They know how to manipulate words and choose the *just right* vocabulary at the *just right* time. Most importantly, "James Dickey's definition of a writer [is] 'someone who is enormously taken by something anyone else would walk by'" (Calkins, p. 3, 1994).

If you haven't practiced writing like this and you don't find pleasure in it, how will you teach children to write like an author? How will you help them to find joy in writing? Sure, it is easy to teach children the bare bones of writing like structures, processes, and rules to follow, but a teacher who is a writer goes beyond this.

Consider what happens when a teacher shows children how to revise vocabulary in their writing. A teacher who does not write often may ask children to use the word wall to find a *million dollar* word to substitute for simple words in their work. However, this type of revision is really about more than replacing one word with another. Someone who practices writing daily will know that.

A teacher who is a writer would not be satisfied with her children finding a word that simply means the same thing. She wants them to find a word that evokes a feeling or connection for the reader, a word that tells the story the best. Someone who hasn't had to grapple with this may give up and not teach children how to search for the *just right* word.

If writing makes you uncomfortable, and you are not confident as a writer, you might have a tendency to rush the writing process. You might not see the important difference between changing out words that are seemingly synonymous and finding the word that describes the magnitude of the situation. Researcher and writing theorist Donald Graves (1994) exemplifies why being a writer is so important for literacy teachers.

> The greatest long-term influence on what the children in your classroom do is your own literacy. The reasons for this are complex. First, when you write with the children, your stance toward learning and the world change. As an active observer, you are more confident of your place in the world. Second, as you continue to work at your writing you create your own long-term inservice for learning better ways to write and teach. Third, you give children the clearest demonstration of the power and function of writing. (p. 154)

In order to build a strong literacy foundation with young children, it is important for you to have a positive relationship with writing. Historically, however, this type of relationship with writing has been hard for teachers to find. Gardner (2014) discovered that very few (1.8 percent) of the 115 student teachers in his study *frequently* wrote for pleasure, with nearly half never finding pleasure in writing. In 2017, Cremin and Oliver conducted a systematic review of empirical research regarding teachers as writers. They found that teachers' attitudes about their own writing, as well as the pedagogy of teaching writing, are negative, with other studies finding negative attitudes for nearly half of those observed (Gardner, 2014).

Teachers link their early school experiences to their view of whether or not they see themselves as a writer (Cremin & Oliver, 2017; Gardner, 2014). For those with negative attitudes toward writing, school-based writing experiences were seen as a task that was too structured, rote, and more secretarial (Gardner, 2014; Draper, Barksdale-Ladd, & Radencich, 2000). This is why it is so important that early childhood teachers understand that teaching choices and attitudes about writing are powerful in shaping who children become as writers.

Whether you already love to write or you see writing as a chore, we want to help you grow as a writer. If you had or still have sparse or intimidating experiences with writing, we want to help you find joy in the process. Begin to explore your relationship with writing by considering these questions:

- When you were a young writer, did you have specific materials and places for writing, or did you write anywhere?
- Was writing a part of your pretend play, something that was fun, or was it more like a chore or an assignment?
- Did you share your writing with others, or was it something that you just kept to yourself?

- Did adults or older family members write for pleasure, or was writing something that they only did to complete a task?
- Did you have teachers who were writers and shared their writing with you, or did your teachers just present procedures when teaching writing?

What did you find out about your history with writing? If you are already a competent writer, then write more. If you found an absence of writing in your early life, commit to building your confidence as a writer. Because you need to be *competent* and *confident* as a writing teacher, it is important for you to commit to being a writer so that you can be a writing model for your children. Take a few minutes to answer these questions:

- Have you had positive experiences with writing, or not?
- Do you feel that you have room to grow as a writer?
- When is the last time you wrote something for fun?

Your answers reflect where you are on your path to being a writing model. If you are not happy with your answers, don't worry. Teachers can improve their ideas about and feelings toward writing and writing instruction. It just takes practice. Start by trying this.

⚠ **Avoid hiding from writing.**

With practice, you will be able to:

- Show what writing feels like, sharing both the ease and struggle
- Motivate children to write, showing a passion for your writing
- Convey confidence, knowing the ins and outs of writing
- Demonstrate that the process is messy, communicating that it takes time and patience

When preservice and inservice teachers engaged in a writing workshop approach, that is, personal writing, topic choice, opportunities to share, experimentation with varied writing styles, and so on, they grew as writers and teachers of writing (Cremin & Oliver, 2017; Gardner, 2014; Locke, Whitehead, & Dix, 2013). "Teachers who perceived themselves as writers offered richer classroom writing experiences and generated increased enjoyment, motivation and tenacity among their students" (Cremin & Oliver, 2017, p. 286).

Like we have said before, it is never too late to learn to love writing and develop as a writer. The quest might not be easy, as it requires first getting over fears and insecurities. Writing evolution takes dedication, like any good pursuit. Remember, writing growth can start with reading.

Finding a passion for reading requires you to read daily (or very close to that). The more we read, the better our chances are of learning to love both reading and writing. Because reading and writing are so interconnected, it is important to make time to read every day and delight in reading and writing.

Appreciate the Significance of Daily Reading

The expert teacher loves reading and is knowledgeable about children's literature. Teachers who are not readers, especially readers of children's literature, will not be able to select the best books for young readers. So, to be that expert teacher of young readers, you have to love the books that you share, you have to know authors and introduce children to the multitude of books that each author writes, and you have to know which books make the best read alouds based on story, language, illustrations, and so on. Figure 1.3 shows some of our favorites that have led to our love of reading.

This is by no means an exhaustive list of the books that we love. Because we read avidly, our list will never be exhausted. Reading daily continues to

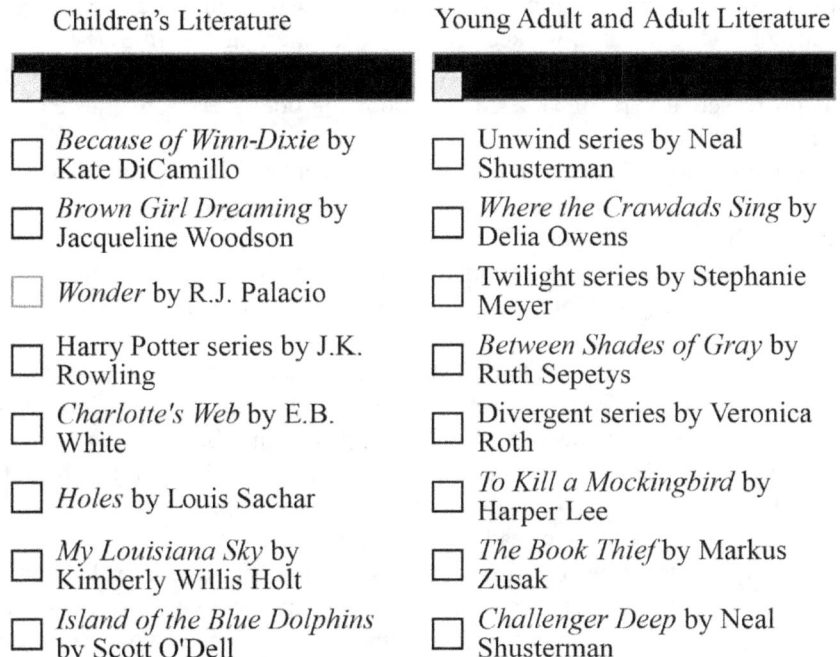

Children's Literature	Young Adult and Adult Literature
☐ *Because of Winn-Dixie* by Kate DiCamillo	☐ Unwind series by Neal Shusterman
☐ *Brown Girl Dreaming* by Jacqueline Woodson	☐ *Where the Crawdads Sing* by Delia Owens
☐ *Wonder* by R.J. Palacio	☐ Twilight series by Stephanie Meyer
☐ Harry Potter series by J.K. Rowling	☐ *Between Shades of Gray* by Ruth Sepetys
☐ *Charlotte's Web* by E.B. White	☐ Divergent series by Veronica Roth
☐ *Holes* by Louis Sachar	☐ *To Kill a Mockingbird* by Harper Lee
☐ *My Louisiana Sky* by Kimberly Willis Holt	☐ *The Book Thief* by Markus Zusak
☐ *Island of the Blue Dolphins* by Scott O'Dell	☐ *Challenger Deep* by Neal Shusterman

Figure 1.3 Some of our favorite books that might help you find a love of reading if you do not know where to begin

grow your list. Think about your own list. Is there a plethora of books on it, or does your list need to grow?

Researchers and literacy professionals acknowledge that you cannot be a good literacy teacher if you don't love to read (Miller, 2009; Powell-Brown, 2004). In her popular book that highlights her literacy-rich classroom where reading choice and a robust library prevail, Donalyn Miller (2009) illustrates her role in sharing a love of reading. "The reason [my students] trust me when I recommend books to them stems from the fact that I read every day of my life and that I talk about reading constantly. I am not mandating an activity for them that I do not engage in myself" (Miller, 2009, Chapter 5, Section 2, loc. 1533).

Unfortunately, studies of preservice and inservice teachers have shown that a majority do not have this love for reading (Miller, 2009; Powell-Brown, 2004). Young readers need teachers who make time to read for pleasure. "If [teachers] make time to read and become engaged in the process it becomes natural, habit-forming behavior" (Powell-Brown, 2004, p. 286).

We know that this may sound daunting to you if you do not read daily. We work with preservice teachers every semester who share that story. But, we don't want you to be intimidated. We want you to be encouraged. Semester after semester, we see preservice teachers move from never having finished a chapter book (and . . . they are juniors in college) to being self-professed lovers of at least one book or book series by the end of fourteen weeks.

We want you to hear from a preservice teacher who reignited her love of reading in one of her teacher education courses (figure 1.4). She shares with you how she fell out of love with reading and why she knew it was essential to rekindle that relationship. Her story is one that we hope will motivate you to get books into your life immediately if you have been neglecting them.

Even if you just start with ten minutes a day before bedtime, you are creating the daily reading habit. That ten minutes will gradually grow into more and more time as you encounter books that just cannot be put down. Before too long, your nightstand will be piled high with books that you just have to read next, and you will not be able to end your day without spending time in a book you have selected to read for enjoyment.

Not only will the time you spend in books foster an affinity for reading, but it also helps you see how authors work as writers. That time you spend in books will impact your view of writing, but remember, in order to grow your relationship with writing, you have to do more than just read your favorite books. You have to write for pleasure and learn to share that writing with others.

 Spotlight on Practice

Kelsey Pierce

Preservice Teacher

My mom *ALWAYS* used to read to me when I was a child, but I didn't read much on my own. By the time I reached high school, my reading had dwindled. I remember a ninth grade English teacher who assigned an essay based on a book. She didn't like the book I chose and made me pick another one, so I no longer was interested in the assignment. It is my *worst* memory of reading. By the time I got to college, I was reading nothing.

I began loving reading again after a teacher education professor pointed out how important it is to read to your class. I thought to myself, I want to have a library like this. I want my children to be engulfed in reading. That professor reignited my passion for reading.

When I have my own classroom, I'm going to have to read to my children daily, no matter what! I hadn't thought about that and realized I need to be reading every day so that I could recommend books to my future students. If I'm not reading the literature, how am I going to recommend a book when the students come and ask me?

My mom recently bought me a Kindle, and I've made it a part of my daily life. I've put reading back into my life by adapting it to what I normally do. Now as an adult, I still picture the stories in my head like I did when I was young, but it's like a little fire got sparked.

I would like to tell teachers to have a passion for reading and show passion for books. A professor's passion for books rubbed off on me. Be a role model for reading. The students will choose books based upon what you show them. If you aren't excited, your children won't be excited about reading. If you show that you are excited about books, show a passion for reading, and show that it's fun, then the children see that.

Figure 1.4 Spotlight on practice: Kelsey Pierce, preservice teacher

Recognize the Importance of Daily Writing

Writing teachers need to understand the craft of writing. Voice, word choice, revision, and development of characters, plot, poetry, informational text, and so on are much more fluid than structured rules that make up mechanics. The mechanics of writing, like spelling, grammar, punctuation, and format, are generally easy to learn, but the craft of writing takes time to hone.

You have to immerse yourself in the more crafty elements of writing. Expert teachers realize that writing evolves as you learn how to mold it so that it represents exactly, down to the independent words, just what a reader wants and needs. You can learn this with practice as you read, write, and pay attention to the ways that stories are told and to the ways that words can move, inspire, and inform readers. Making this practice a daily habit is imperative for building a strong relationship with writing.

What if you start to hone your craft and build your love of writing by exploring some of your favorite authors? Those authors have mastered craft; they are great models for both you and your children. While there are many children's book authors who are experts at their craft, table 1.1 shows some of our favorite excerpts that inspire us as writers.

Table 1.1 These examples show the craft that adds depth and interest to these pieces of text.

Book	Quote	Context
Thank You, Mr. Falker by Patricia Polacco (1998, unpaged picture storybook)	"But it was not long after that night that her grandma must have let go of the grass, because she went to where the lights were, on the other side."	Powerful, yet subtle, crafting of words to show that a character died, evoking contemplation about the gravity of what just happened
Out of My Mind by Sharon Draper (2012, chapter book)	"My mother whispered her strength into my ear" (p. 2).	Eloquence of craft, where the author used words to create a visual representation of a mother's love, describing how a mother empowered a daughter who cannot walk or talk—and never will
The One and Only Ivan by Katherine Applegate (2012, chapter book)	"Sometimes I press my nose against the glass. My noseprint, like your fingerprint, is the first and last and only one. The man wipes the glass and then I am gone" (p. 14).	An artful way to organize and choose simple vocabulary to show how insignificant, lost, and lonely Ivan, the gorilla, felt in his enclosure; "I am gone" hangs in the air, leaving the reader with a sense of great sadness for Ivan.
Finding Winnie: The True Story of the World's Most Famous Bear by Lindsay Mattick (2015, unpaged nonfiction picture book)	"On the train platform was a man on a bench with a baby. 'A baby?' said Cole, annoyed. A baby bear. A cub."	The artful weaving of two modes: narrative nonfiction and dialogic memoir (italicized) to tell the amazing true story about how Winnie-the-Pooh came to be.

After reading these excerpts, what are your thoughts about how these authors crafted their texts? Once you begin to investigate more models, you will want to practice to see if you can mimic their work or create your style that is just as powerful. Research has shown us that teachers can grow as writers and teachers of writing when they intentionally practice.

Think about it this way. If you aren't the writer that you want to be, now is the time to begin to consider how to put yourself on a path where writing can be easily integrated into your life: *read, write,* and *share.*

- *Read* some of your favorite children's literature and begin to evaluate what those authors do that make their writing so good. "The writing you get out of your students can only be as good as the classroom literature that surrounds and sustains it" (Fletcher & Portalupi, 1998, p. 10).
- *Write* for pleasure. You have to find what makes writing pleasurable for you. Just because your friends keep a journal doesn't mean that you have to keep a journal. Journaling might not be your thing. Perhaps what brings you joy is writing little stories about your children every day or taking the ordinary, like a trip to the grocery store, and making it into some extraordinary story. Be open-minded about what you choose to write for pleasure.
- *Share* your writing with other people. Start by sharing with someone you trust so that they can gently guide you on how to grow your writing. When you feel more *competent* and *confident*, begin to share with others. Writers need feedback to thrive.

Our second Spotlight on Practice with Gabe and Anna Silveira (figure 1.5) will give you an idea of what a flourishing writing life might look like, even when that early writing life might have been hindered by strict school practices. Their story is one that shows you how dissimilar writers are, yet how *competent* and *confident* they can be with those differences.

Gabe and Anna both found their way to being teachers who are writers, but the paths that they took to get there were very different. They support each other as writers, sharing their writing freely. They honor their difference in writing styles, and this has translated into their work with children as well. Their experiences have influenced who they are as writers and teachers of writing. Perhaps these tips from Gabe and Anna will help you grow as a writer and a writing teacher:

- Find your mood for writing, and write while *mooding*.
- Recognize your own process.
- The struggle is real, and it is ok to let children know that you still struggle or leave a piece unfinished to return to tomorrow.

Spotlight on Practice

Gabe & Anna Silveira

Fourth-Grade Teacher and Administrator

Finding My Writing Voice

Gabe: My writing practice felt spoon-fed; I just tried to do what the smart kids were doing. Most teachers taught the writing process in a linear way (first prewrite, then draft, then revise, then edit). I hated prewriting because I like to start in the middle of my story and work out the beginning and end from there. School completely took away from the joy of writing.

When I was in my teacher education program, I had a teacher who told me that I was a writer! Now, I focus on writing the way I want. I start in unconventional places and move pieces of the story around. My journey has taught me that writing teachers have to stop holding children accountable to rigid ways of solving things and give them freedom to flex their creative muscles.

Anna: My dad is an author; my mother is his editor. I have always known that I am a writer. My family and I wrote for fun at home. But, I also had trouble with the way writing was taught in school. I remember faking spelling and grammar mistakes just to have errors to fix on revision day. I enjoy writing, even writing lesson plans, simply because it is writing. But, teaching writing is intimidating for me. I had to learn to trust kids and let them have their own process. My experience stretched my understanding of how emerging writers work.

Our Writing Lives

Gabe: I met Anna at a birthday party and got to know her better through her Facebook posts. I became more and more infatuated by her because of the way she wrote. When dating, the two of us even exchanged a journal where we shared our feelings. Now, Anna regularly uses writing to vocalize her views in a blog and is writing a children's book. She writes while multitasking, phone in one hand and our baby in the other. Then, she shares it all with me.

Anna: Gabe is also writing a children's book and writes professionally; he needs a couple of hours alone to write, usually in another room. Speaking to each other is not enough. Writing is cathartic, an outlet; it's perfect.

Figure 1.5 Spotlight on practice: Gabe and Anna Silveira, fourth-grade teacher and administrator

- Writing can be intimidating, but you are in the same position as most of your children. Just experience it with them, and share discoveries as they happen; learn from these.
- Be the cheerleader that you have always wanted and needed. Pay attention to what you tell yourself when you write. Your kids might do that too. It'll help you find your voice.

- Read a lot. Find a community of readers who are interested in what you like to read as well. This also means having more than one community that reads and thinks differently. You're allowed to be a part of more than one community, especially if they disagree with each other.
- Write a lot. Find a community of writers filled with people you know and don't know. Curate a panel of expert writers and mentors to discuss advanced ideas. Tolkien and Lewis had this; no one writes in a vacuum. Create an arena of support for yourself and your kiddos.
- Listen a lot. Find podcasts about books and writing; listen to books on Audible.
- Celebrate progress.

So, make choices that inspire you to write daily, but start small if this feels intimidating. Give yourself freedom to write in a way that is gratifying to you. Open yourself up to reading children's literature widely and savoring the words of the authors. Share your love for writing; write with colleagues, commit to writing, and experience the joy that writing can bring into your own life. All of this will help you grow as a writer and a writing teacher.

Ease into Daily Reading and Writing

You don't have to read or write 1,000 pages a day to fall in love with reading and writing. The journey into daily reading and writing doesn't have to be difficult. Gradually ease yourself into the world of reading and writing.

You can read about children's books, learn about books and writing from authors, and even publish your own writing. For example, you could subscribe to blogs, connect to websites, follow authors and teachers on Twitter, or download podcasts that will introduce you to avid readers, authors, and a plethora of the latest and greatest book titles.

Start with the *Nerdy Book Club* blog. This is a space where teachers, authors, and researchers can write about the power of children's and young adult literature. Colby Sharp and Donalyn Miller, along with Teacher Learning Sessions, started *The Nerdy Bookcast* podcast where they interview authors and book talk outstanding book titles. Colby and Travis Jonkers host a podcast called *The Yarn*, where they talk with authors about their latest books, their experiences talking to readers, and their writing process. While you are finding new books to read, you are also learning about the craft of writing from authors.

For a great podcast that focuses just on children's books and authors, *The Children's Book Podcast* is a fantastic resource that is hosted by school librarian Matthew Winner. Matthew has hundreds of podcast interviews with authors. Donalyn (@donalynbooks), Colby (@colbysharp), Travis (@100scopenotes), and Matthew (@MatthewWinner) also have excellent Twitter feeds full of information, and they sometimes give away free books. Finally, check out websites like *All the Wonders* for links to videos, books, and crafts. You can also start your own blogs or Twitter feeds where you write about what you are reading, your teaching experiences, and more, which will help sharpen your writing skills.

Beyond podcasts and blogs there are various lists available that point teachers to quality children's literature. The American Library Association (ALA), www.ala.org, awards children's literature for written content and illustration. The Newbery Medal is awarded to the most distinguished piece of American children's literature. It is the most well-known author award in the world, and these books provide the perfect mentors to help you with your writing craft. In addition, the Caldecott Award is given for illustrations in American children's picture books. Both the Newbery (1922–present) and Caldecott (1938–present) lists are available on the ALA website.

Use these lists to challenge yourself to read a picture book a day. Keep a chapter book on your nightstand, and read just a few minutes before bed. Maybe even jot a few notes about what you are reading, making a list of titles, capturing vocabulary or beautifully composed sentences, and noting your responses to important events that happen in the plot. Think about it this way. By only spending a few minutes each day with your book and your notes, you can build your relationship with reading and writing in a nonthreatening way.

You can also take some time to get to know *A Writer's Notebook: Unlocking the Writer Within You* by Ralph Fletcher. It is an easy read, originally written for children, that will help you understand the writer's notebook, a place where you can write interesting things that people say and do or things that make you wonder. You can draw and glue in pictures of funny, sad, or significant events, people, or places. It's a place for lists, both practical and dreams. The point is that the writer's notebook allows you to capture many, many little seeds.

So, try it. Keep a writer's notebook. Eventually, you can go back and investigate those little seeds and work on adding more to help them grow into something bigger. The writer's notebook gives you space to safely navigate writer's craft.

When you have eased into writing in your personal space at home, take the leap into writing with others. Remember, sharing and getting feedback about your writing will help you grow and develop a love of writing. Try this on for size: Participate in a writing workshop experience, like the National Writing Project. You will be surprised by how your entire outlook on writing will change and how much more confident you will be.

These resources can change your life if you need to enhance your love of reading and writing. They will also help you become an expert on children's literature and author's craft simultaneously. Your students need you to have a wide knowledge of children's literature and the craft of writing; they need you to help them love reading and writing. The only way for you to truly have this knowledge is to be in love with those books and to have *confidence* and *competence* in your own writing. Your love of literacy will ultimately grow lifelong readers and writers. It's that important!

Principle 2

Build a Library of Books

When you are a teacher who is a reader and writer, it is only natural that you will be enthusiastic about sharing books with children. As a lover of books, you will have a lot of them in both your home and in your classroom. The idea of a classroom library isn't something foreign to someone who loves to read and write.

All classrooms should have a library, a comfortable place where children and teachers feel at home with books. Imagine:

- A variety of books that are easy to access and are displayed in baskets and on shelves
- Bean bags and pillows strewn across a shag carpet
- A lamp casting a soft light across the area
- Pictures of authors and quotes about reading covering the walls
- Kids curled up with books, reading silently or quietly talking about them

In this library, reading happens naturally.

TALK ABOUT THE CLASSROOM LIBRARY

Listen as two second-grade children explore a classroom library (figure 2.1). How is the classroom library benefiting the children? What do the children know about books? How does the library promote dialogue about reading?

Cade and Hunter are able to use the classroom library to find books for independent reading. Clearly, the library is robust and contains many books, including both fiction and nonfiction. The boys have knowledge of book titles and are obviously readers who know what they like to read. Their

Cade: Hey, look at this one. It's called *Giant Squid*. Look at that thing on the cover? It's creepy.

Hunter: Oh, I read that one. Wait until you see the page about its beak and gross tongue. It's cool. You would like that one since you like to read about animals.

Cade: Oh, great. I think I will read it. What are you going to choose?

Hunter: I'm not sure. I just finished the last Spiderwick Chronicles book.

Cade: What's that about?

Hunter: It's about kids who discover a secret world where they battle these magical creatures.

Cade: Wait! I liked *Christmas in Camelot*. It had magic, and the characters have to complete a mission. You might like it. Oh, here it is. See, it's a part of the Magic Tree House books.

Hunter: Ok, give me that one. I'll try it.

Figure 2.1 A little talk about the classroom library

conversation shows that they remember what they have read and feel comfortable recommending books. They know how to browse the library and talk about reading, just like most adults do. This is a sophisticated behavior that teachers can promote with classroom libraries like the one previously described.

Libraries like these might seem intimidating or even non-obtainable, but the truth is that teachers can build spaces where children have easy access to large varieties of books. In this principle, you will learn why classroom libraries are so important and tips for building them.

VISUALIZE YOUR CLASSROOM LIBRARY

Many teachers create classroom libraries with a series of shelves lining one classroom wall; those shelves are bursting with books of all genres and topics. Can you picture the colorful spines, books of different sizes and shapes, covers facing out on top of the shelves, and so on?

We want you to see those shelves as an integral part of your *core* classroom library. That library will promote:

- Variety in your read alouds
- Opportunity for impromptu, *alongside* reading

- Choice for children's independent reading
- Intriguing conversations about a wide variety of topics and life lessons

What might be a little unusual is the way that we ask you to extend your thinking about the classroom library.

Because literacy should be infused throughout the day in the early childhood classroom, we want to propose a core classroom library in the traditional sense but with *sublibraries* that can be integrated in all subject areas and in whole group, small group, and independent learning experiences. What do we mean by sublibraries? Think about these possibilities:

- Tubs of books to accompany each learning area
- Big book storage for shared reading, used by both the teacher and children
- Usable displays full of student-created books that can be read and reread (Tip: use classroom materials or visit free websites like www.lulu.com to make books.)
- Leveled books organized and stored in an area for teacher use when teaching targeted skills to small groups or individuals.
- Baskets or a designated shelf for books that have been recently read aloud

⚠ **Avoid having children focus on levels. Book levels are for teachers, not for students.**

All of those sublibraries are important and can be built from the larger core library that lines your wall, book rooms in schools, or school or community libraries. These sublibraries can be very fluid, changing based on skills and content and, of course, children's interest.

We would like to challenge you to broaden the way you have always defined a classroom library. Think about how you can build that important wall of books but also expand that wall out to other areas of your classroom.

KNOW THE IMPORTANCE OF A CLASSROOM LIBRARY

From the way we have defined it, the core classroom library, at the very least, has the potential to put books in the hands of students. That, in and of itself, is super important. After all, if children do not have access to books, then they cannot read them.

Classroom libraries, comprised of a core library and sublibraries, put books within easy reach of young children. "Study after study proves that physical access to books makes the difference" (Miller & Sharp, 2018, p. 8). Neuman (1999) highlights this point in a study with classrooms of three- and four-year-olds in low-socioeconomic communities with poor classroom libraries.

Teachers in the control group acquired books (5 books × number of children in the class) that matched the needs and interests of their children. They were trained on read alouds and story/content integration and introduced to local libraries. The literacy interactions between these teachers and their children almost doubled, and the teachers were more likely to read often and widely to groups and individuals. The 400 children in the experimental group performed statistically significantly higher on literacy assessments and held those gains when reassessed six months later in kindergarten.

Having more books in the classroom positively impacts teacher interactions and academic performance of children. "Children need rich and diverse reading materials to acquire the complex set of attitudes, skills, and behaviors associated with literacy development" (Neuman, 1999, p. 306). Linking position statements of the two major literacy organizations in the United States, International Literacy Association (ILA, 2018; IRA, 2014) and National Council of Teachers of English (NCTE, 2017), reveals that giving children access to books for independent reading has the potential to impact:

- Reading achievement
- Reading comprehension
- Language/Vocabulary
- Motivation/Attitude
- Time reading
- Empathy

This is by no means an exhaustive list of the research-based evidence. It does, however, show the importance of access to books. In addition to the academic benefits, the classroom library encourages inquisitive conversations about books. Children explore; they go deeper into their interests. They get more practice with reading because their hands are on books every day.

BUILD IT, AND THEY WILL READ

Use What You Have to Get Books

You are going to need books—lots of books! While the research varies about the exact number of books a classroom library should have, at the very least it should "include a minimum of 300 titles and up to 1,000 books or more" in every classroom (Miller & Sharp, 2018, p. 36). There should be:

- Duplicate copies of favorites
- Books that represent the diversity of each classroom each year

- Books that are not only on children's instructional levels but also some that are a few above and below
- Books that are new and currently popular
- Multiple genres of books
- Electronic books
- Periodicals
- Audio books

We understand. You are probably thinking that you will have to buy all of these books. Take a deep breath. You shouldn't have to buy all of the books for the classroom library. Here are ways to get books at minimal cost.

Research your area to determine if there is a community or school library. Not every community or school has one, but a large majority do. The downside is that you have to return the books, so they cannot be a permanent part of the classroom library. But, until you have your own books, borrowing books is the next best thing.

Every year you meet a new group of students who have different interests, and throughout the year, those interests change. The community or school library gives you flexibility to change books as often as you need, and it doesn't cost anything except for your time. These libraries often have a variety of books (paper, electronic, hard cover). Some libraries even allow teachers to check out 100 books or more for multiple weeks, so the children have plenty of time to peruse and use the books. In addition, they are generally staffed by someone knowledgeable about books, so librarians can help you find the *just right* books for your students.

Some schools have book rooms that are shared by all of the teachers in the school. These rooms sometimes contain sets of leveled books for direct instruction, big books for shared reading, or sets of high interest texts for book clubs or literature circles. While these books wouldn't supplement your core classroom library, they would be valuable for some of your sublibraries.

Talk to your administrators about how funding can enhance book purchases. Sometimes your school may give you a budget for purchasing books for your classroom library. Take the lead in helping select books for book rooms. Let your school librarian know what books are typically of interest to your students. If your school does not budget for books in a way that is best for children, do not be afraid to lobby for books.

Acquire the Rest Creatively

Regardless of your book budget, remember to seek out inexpensive ways to accrue books for the classroom library. Grants, discounted book sales, and donations are good places to start.

Write Grants

You can write small grants for the purpose of purchasing books for the classroom. Any amount is helpful in building a library. Check with your school district, city council, local businesses, and so on to determine if there are grants or donations available. These are often easy to acquire and not as intimidating as when you apply for larger, national grants. Simply make a little time for writing, and don't be afraid of them.

You can get the most bang for your buck with grants because they are often cash value, which means that you can buy the books that you know your students need. The grants can be tailored to fit the individual needs of your students and classroom library. So, start small with local grants and then expand your thinking to bigger funding like those listed in table 2.1.

We encourage you to do an extensive search for grants because there are too many out there to list here. The possibilities really are very vast. You will be surprised by how much of your classroom library can be built from grant awards.

Find Discounted or Free Books

Discounted book sales can be a great place for finding resources to start your classroom library, add titles, or replace worn-out books. While we understand that authors may not get royalties from some discounted book sellers, these businesses provide teachers with affordable options for bringing large quantities of books into the classroom. The important thing is to get books

Table 2.1   An initial list of resources for grant funding

Grants	
National Education Association Student Achievement	http://www.nea.org/grants
NEA Foundation Education	https://www.neafoundation.org/for-educators/student-achievement-grants/
Scholastic Literacy	https://www.scholastic.com/teachers/articles/teaching-content/teachers-get-grant/
Junior Library Guild Book	https://www.juniorlibraryguild.com/grants/
Book Love Foundation Classroom Library	booklovefoundation.org/apply
National Home Library Foundation	http://homelibraryfoundation.org/
The Snapdragon Book Foundation	https://snapdragonbookfoundation.org/
International Book Project	https://www.intlbookproject.org/home/our-work/get-books-2/
Kids Need to Read	http://community.kidsneedtoread.org/

Table 2.2   Discounted book resources: A place to start your search for economical books.

Discounted Book Sales	
Scholastic Book Club	https://clubs.scholastic.com/
Scholastic Book Fair	http://www.scholastic.com/bookfairs/
Scholastic Warehouse Sales	https://bookfairs.scholastic.com/bookfairs/events/warehouse-sales.html
Brick-and-mortar resale bookstores (like Half Price Books in Texas)	Do an online search for shops in your area.
Online resale bookstores	thriftbooks.com, betterworldbooks.com, ebay.com, amazon.com, etc.
Garage sales, thrift stores (like Goodwill), etc.	Find these locally.
Public library	They often sell books for $1.00 or less as they are replacing old books with newer copies.

in children's hands first, spark that love of reading, and then, children will be more likely to buy new books by their favorite authors. Take a look at table 2.2 for a few options to get you started on a grand classroom library.

As you can see, Scholastic has many options for discounted books. Remember those book orders you used to get from them? Scholastic now has an online ordering system. Parents can peruse the catalogs online, easily access the teacher's account, and pay with a credit card. You do not have to count order forms or keep track of money, but you can still receive points that can be used to buy books for the classroom.

Scholastic can also set up a book fair at your school where teachers, children, and parents can purchase books at discounted rates to add to the classroom. Their warehouse sales are popular events where you buy one book and get one free. There are no limits on the number of books that you can buy. In addition, you can work at the warehouse sales and receive discounts on your purchases, all tax exempt. These usually happen twice a year in major cities. Be sure to regularly check their website for specific event dates/times.

Beyond large companies like Scholastic, you might have to do a little extra legwork to find discounted book resources near you. You can look for stores in your area and online where you can purchase books. When books become old, tattered, or no longer wanted, some resale stores will buy the books back, and you can get store credit to purchase other titles. Don't forget about garage sales and thrift stores. It may take a little more time to find the *just right* books but can cheaply provide you with great results.

A final option is that you might look for ways to have books donated. Teachers who are retiring are often looking for a new home for their books. Before parents discard any books, encourage them to donate to you, and remind them that you can always exchange books that might not fit the library with other teachers, discount bookstores, and so on. How about posting a teacher wish list outside your classroom door or on any website you use to communicate with parents? You could even provide a QR code or link to your Amazon wish list where parents can work to clear your cart for you.

Another idea is to have parents donate a child's favorite book to the classroom as a birthday celebration. In lieu of cupcakes or cookies, a special ceremony can be held for the induction of the book into the classroom library, and a name card can be placed in the book so that the student who donated it can always be remembered. You can read the book to the class before it is shelved.

Now that we have given you a few ideas, can you think of other ways to grow a classroom library? When do you plan to start getting books for your library? While accumulating books is definitely fun, be sure your collection is both broad and deep with variety.

ACQUIRE A VARIETY OF BOOKS

A classroom library should be flexible based on the students' wants and needs. NCTE (2017) states that "we know that no book is right for every student, and classroom libraries offer ongoing opportunities for you to work with students as individuals to find books that will ignite their love for learning, calm their fears, answer their questions, and improve their lives in any of the multiple ways that only literature can" (para. 2). Because of this, the classroom library is always in flux. Because of this, your classroom library will need to be broad, including books that represent:

- Multiple genres, like realistic fiction, fantasy, historical fiction, biography, memoir, informational books, poetry
- Multiple structures, like narrative, expository, graphic/illustration, verse
- Multiple modes, like picture storybooks, wordless picture books, big books, easy readers, chapter books, periodicals/articles, reference books, eBooks, audio books
- Multiple cultures and topics, like those representative of both the children in your classroom and those children who might be very different from them

Joni Martino's classroom library (figure 2.2) is an example of this. One major section of the library has categories that are of interest to second-grade children, and the books within those categories offer breadth, including both fiction and nonfiction.

Figure 2.2 Joni Martino's classroom library has a variety of texts

Most teachers really love fiction. So, having a collection of good fictional stories, fairy tales, fables, and other fantastical literature is not hard for most of us. Poetry, with its rhyme, rhythm, and often lyrical nature, is an early childhood teacher's *go-to* choice for enhancing oral language and phonological awareness development. Nonfiction, on the other hand, is often neglected, but it shouldn't be.

Yopp and Yopp (2006) found that only 8 percent of the books chosen for read alouds in preschool classrooms in their study were informational books. In another study related to nonfiction books in first-grade classrooms, researchers found statistically significantly enhanced comprehension and vocabulary learning, as well as motivation for reading informational texts, when compared to direct instruction with fiction (Kuhn, Raush, McCarty, Montgomery, & Rule, 2017). When classroom libraries include fiction, poetry, *and* nonfiction trade books, a love for all genres can grow and literacy learning is improved. Classroom libraries have to be purposeful in their inclusion of nonfiction.

When we were younger, we didn't have classroom libraries. Nonfiction books were almost nonexistent and were dry with *just the facts*. Nonfiction was for writing research papers or reports; it wasn't for curious exploring or inquiry. We didn't use trade books to supplement learning about history; we just used textbooks.

Now, nonfiction is much different. Authors are creating informational books with attractive images and intriguing material about topics that are of great interest to kids. Consider Chris Barton's *Whoosh! Lonnie Johnson's Super-soaking Stream of Inventions*. This book uses the topic of a water gun to show young readers a positive story about an African American inventor and engineer who found great success in his ability to take risks.

Or, think about how Melissa Sweet, award-winning illustrator, uses vibrant color and naïve images to invite in young readers. Jen Bryant's *A Splash of Red: The Life and Art of Horace Pippin* is a great example of how Sweet uses illustrations that entice readers so they can experience a story of triumph after adversity, while also developing an appreciation for art.

Nonfiction books are no longer the dry bones facts that we used to know; they are vibrant and varied. They are sometimes written in beautiful narrative or shared through insightful memoir. Both authors and publishers are much more in tune with the audience, and, as a result, nonfiction will be a very popular addition to your classroom library.

In addition to assuring that you have variety in genres, make sure that you don't depend too much on your favorite formats. Children love picture storybooks; early childhood classrooms often abound with these, and they should. They are great for read alouds, for centers, and for independent reading experiences for young children. But, don't forget chapter books, periodicals, and books in electronic formats. Chapter books like Mary Pope Osborne's Magic Tree House series or classics like E.B. White's *Stuart Little* provide treasured read aloud experiences in early childhood classrooms.

But, what about thinking outside of the book? Young children are curious and love to learn interesting information from periodicals. They also love listening to books and reading them in electronic formats. *Time for Kids* has news articles perfect for K-2 classrooms. You can even search for topics specific to classroom library need.

Classroom libraries can be supplemented with audio and e-books, which can serve as *alongside* reading partners when you cannot be close by. Students can listen to books while following along or use the functions in an e-book to assist with decoding skills during independent reading. McNelly (2018) recommends e-books that:

- Are easy for independent use
- Have options for individualization
- Provide methods for scaffolding reading
- Have nothing that distracts from the act of reading

The classroom library should also have depth. While you will want to have popular series books and controlled texts that are easier for new readers, a large portion of the books should be authentic. "Authentic text is real, living language written to engage readers and draw them in; it may entertain, inform, or persuade. It invites active reading, robust problem-solving, and deep analysis because it comprises conceptually rich, compelling ideas and language from life" (Bridges, 2018, para. 2).

Think about the difference between Dr. Seuss's *Mr. Brown Can Moo, Can You?* and Audrey Penn's *The Kissing Hand*. We need Mr. Brown in the library because it offers fun, colorful illustrations, and great practice with phonological awareness and phonics. But, it is missing story, the thing that makes us question and ponder and feel.

We need Penn's book so that children understand story structure and character development. Her book also asks children to explore their feelings about the first day of school. It gives opportunities for more robust conversations, while Seuss's book provides playful interactions with language skills. Both are important. Since our children will one day grow into readers who explore books outside of those with simple form and function, the classroom library should have a larger percentage of authentic books.

Multicultural books are great options for adding depth to your classroom library. Books that explore people, places, and cultures are usually authentic. They give children insight and allow them to live vicariously through the stories of others. Children grow to understand other cultures and draw closer to those who are different. Matt de la Peña's *Last Stop on Market Street* depicts multigenerational relationships, altruism, people of color, and a main character who learns to see value in those who are different from him.

Think broadly about what multicultural books could include. There are many types of differences: age, race, gender, ability, cities, countries, and more. Make sure that you have chosen authentic multicultural books with rich storylines. The books should avoid stereotypes in both words and illustrations, be meaningful in terms of teaching life lessons, and offer the opportunity for appreciation of differences. Having a large variety of multicultural books in your library provides wisdom children need to grow into open-minded citizens.

When ensuring that your classroom library is both broad and deep, the resources in table 2.3 might be helpful in your search.

Having a classroom library requires you to stay current with children's books and stay *in the know* about your children's interests.

> We believe that the moment we begin to feel comfortable or confident in our collections or start thinking we are doing everything necessary or that can be done to create a library of diverse representations and texts is the moment in which we need to remind ourselves that this type of work is never done. (Crisp et al., 2016, p. 39)

Table 2.3 Resources for finding varied books that add depth and breadth to your classroom library

Multicultural Book Resources	
Cooperative Children's Book Center (50 books every child should know, divided by age groups)	http://ccbc.education.wisc.edu/books/detailListBooks.asp?idBookLists=42
Dolly Gray Children's Literature Award (from the Division on Autism and Developmental Disabilities)	dollygrayaward.com/
Notable Books for a Global Society (from ILA's Children's Literature & Reading Special Interest Group)	clrsig.org/notable-books-for-a-global-society-nbgs.html
Once Upon a World Children's Book Award (from the Simon Wiesenthal Center)	http://www.wiesenthal.com/about/library-and-archives/once-upon-a-world-childrens-book-award.html
Periodical Resources	
Time for Kids (search by grade level)	https://www.timeforkids.com/
DOGO News for Kids (search by grade level)	https://www.dogonews.com/
Scholastic News Magazine (for purchase)	https://scholasticnews.scholastic.com/
Newsela (search lower elementary)	https://newsela.com/
Fiction and Nonfiction Book Resources	
Orbis Pictus Award (best children's nonfiction)	https://www2.ncte.org/awards/orbis-pictus-award-nonfiction-for-children/
NCTE Children's Book Awards	https://www2.ncte.org/blog/2018/11/2019-book-awards/
Notable Children's Books by the Association for Library Service to Children (ALSC)	http://www.ala.org/alsc/awardsgrants/notalists/ncb

Consider what second-grade teacher Joni Martino has to say about her classroom library and staying *in the know* (figure 2.3). And, as you add new titles to your classroom library, create a space that invites children to be *in the know* as well.

ARRANGE THE CLASSROOM LIBRARY SPACE

Get to know each year's class *before* ordering new books for the classroom library and sublibraries. Neuman (2001) recommends that you have books that are core to your library, remaining the same, and books that rotate in and out of your library every few weeks. Don't forget; this applies to the sublibraries as well. The idea is that your classroom library should change with the needs of the children and curriculum.

Spotlight on Practice

Joni Martino

Second-Grade Teacher

I actually have two classroom library areas with numbered tubs of books labeled and organized by author, topic, genre, and more. All kids even have their own book bins so they can choose the books they want to read. Children use the library every day during the Read to Self station time and during arrival before morning announcements begin. There are math tubs so kids can read about math during math stations and mentor texts for social studies and science when kids are curious and want to know more. Anything can be taught with a good book. If I can tie it to a book, I know I can reach my kids.

To make sure that children continue to use the classroom library, I stay current in what's popular. I am constantly adding and sometimes grouping books differently. I also have to evaluate to find out if certain books are relevant, like series books because they can come and go.

In the beginning, I shopped garage sales and used bookstores. I have always done scholastic book orders, which helps me get free books. If someone is giving away books, I take them. My father-in-law has even cleared my Amazon cart on my birthday. I have used the website Donor's Choose and get grants from my school district to purchase new books. I never turn down a book!

I introduce how to choose books, put books back, and read labels. I read books aloud and tell children what bins to look in to find a particular book or other books like it. Kids can explore and find books that speak to them, books that they want to read. Every kid reads every day!

The library is the center of my room; my class revolves around it. Our classroom library does not limit them to a section or level. It is where I meet with kids, connect with them, and where I share my love for books. I want them to be surrounded by books, or like I once heard someone say, "hugged by books."

Figure 2.3   Spotlight on practice: Joni Martino, second-grade teacher

Highlight Books by Topic

Young, Moss, and Cornwell (2007) suggest organizing the library by topic, rather than genre, which increases student interest and promotes reading. For example, a section of the core library or a sublibrary in a center could be dedicated to a topic that is currently all the rage with your children. Isabel McHan's (Spotlight on practice teacher, Principle 4) prekindergarten students became interested in the Great Wall of China after hearing from a guest speaker; her students wanted to know everything they could about the country, building walls, the culture, and more.

Labeling a section of your library with a specific topic, like China, can satisfy and fuel curiosity.

Early childhood classrooms typically have books organized by many topics that are of interest to children. But, some of your books may not fit into these categories or may not be of specific interest at that time. Having these books organized by genre will make the library well rounded and balanced and help facilitate understanding of the different types of books. But, how do you make the topics or genres visible and make it easy for students to find and replace books?

1. Determine the topic: if the children are interested in NASA, create a sublibrary (or a space for it in the core library if not being used in a center).
2. Figure out where the books for that topic will be placed: the books will be in a tub in the NASA dramatic play center.
3. Choose a color that will represent the topic: the tub is blue, so that will be the color to represent NASA.
4. Create a picture as a label so that children can find the topic: a space shuttle drawn by two children in the class is attached to the blue tub.
5. Add books about the topic: fiction, nonfiction, periodicals, and so on related to space, NASA, astronauts, space stations, and more are added to the blue tub.
6. Color code books: since the tub is blue, place a small blue sticker on the front cover of the books in the tub (put all stickers in the same location, like the upper-right corner; removable/reusable stickers might be good because some of the books may be used in a different area later).

Make the Space Comfortable

The classroom library has to be an inviting place for reading and exploration. It should be tidy and bright, a comfortable place. It should invite children to browse and spend time with books. They should have time to contemplate, pull books from the shelf or tub, read a little, and put it back. Get creative with the design of the space. Make it your own, but remember to use what you already have before spending money in your budget. Here are ideas to get you started:

- Soft lighting, like lamps, because fluorescent lighting is not optimal for all readers
- Soft furnishings (bean bags, pillows, couches, etc.) so that readers can get comfortable like they would at home

- Soft flooring, like rugs or interlocking mats so children have a cozy place to spread out

Displaying book covers and jackets is another way to invite children into books. Students should be able to see the titles and illustrations, so think about placement of books so that there are more than book spines visible. Be creative with shelving that allows books to be displayed. Some teachers have hung plastic rain gutters low along walls as a way to display books with covers facing out. Google "plastic rain gutters as classroom bookshelves," and you will see many examples. So, start paying close attention to books with the most attractive illustrations on the covers or interesting titles, along with classroom favorites. Then, display these to spark children's interests.

Figure 2.4 gives an example of a space where children can feel comfortable. They can browse labeled tubs and shelves with books and sit comfortably on carpet or soft movable seating. It is organized and invites children to read.

Figure 2.4 Another section of Joni Martino's classroom library

CREATE SYSTEMS FOR USING THE LIBRARY

Get the kids involved in organizing your classroom library. Have them help create easy systems for checking out and reshelving books. Consider Donalyn Miller's idea for *Shelfies*, where children use iPads to take pictures of themselves with selected books when they are checking them out; the photo is deleted when the books are returned (Miller & Sharp, 2018). Catapano, Fleming, and Elias (2009) recommend having children write names on an item like a paint stirrer. When they remove a book from a shelf or a tub, children place the paint stirrer where the book goes for easy return.

There are also apps that allow children to use a device, like an iPad or a computer, to easily check books in and out. Booksource Classroom and Classroom Checkout are two free options. Even very young children can take responsibility for tracking books, and you can view details about classroom library use. You should try to find methods to track reading habits, choices, books tried and put back, responses to books, and so on. Remember, it is not all about finding lost books; it's about how children use the library and engage with reading.

As your library gets love from your children, it might show a little wear and tear. So, to keep the library fresh, consider removing tired and tattered books and replacing them with new copies. Remove books that no longer attract students. Add new titles based on interest. Make sure the children are very involved in this process. Let them determine what books are removed and added. Introduce the new books by either book talks or read alouds, and let the children decide where new books should go in the library.

Teach Children about the Library

Now that you have the library set up and functional, teach the children how to use it. Here are some tips that will help your children treat the library with care and use it in the most effective way:

- Decide on the rules for library use. Create these with the children. Make charts with icons to accompany the written rules. The children can help draw those icons.
- Model how to use the library. Show the children how their rules work and how to care for books. Children need to see examples of books that have been loved and those that have not. They need to know simple ways to repair books. Consider creating a little first-aid kit for books that includes tapes, erasers, glue, and so on.

- Practice using the library, gradually releasing the children to explore it. Open small sections of the core library or one sublibrary and have small groups of children rotate through, giving them time to explore and practice library etiquette.

The idea is to give the children ownership as much as possible. Use a lot of picture-based anchor charts created as a class to help them. Allow for flexibility in the charts as the children learn more about their library and want to make changes to the library rules. Figure 2.5 gives you an idea of what this can look like in early childhood classrooms.

If we want children to read, we need to reward them with books. Studies have proven this (Marinak & Gambrell, 2008). The classroom library provides the reward. "Students who have access to a collection of quality books in their classrooms read 50%–60% more than students who do not have access" (ILA, 2018, p. 6). How do you get your children to read more? It's the LIBRARY, so do not forget what the children need you to do:

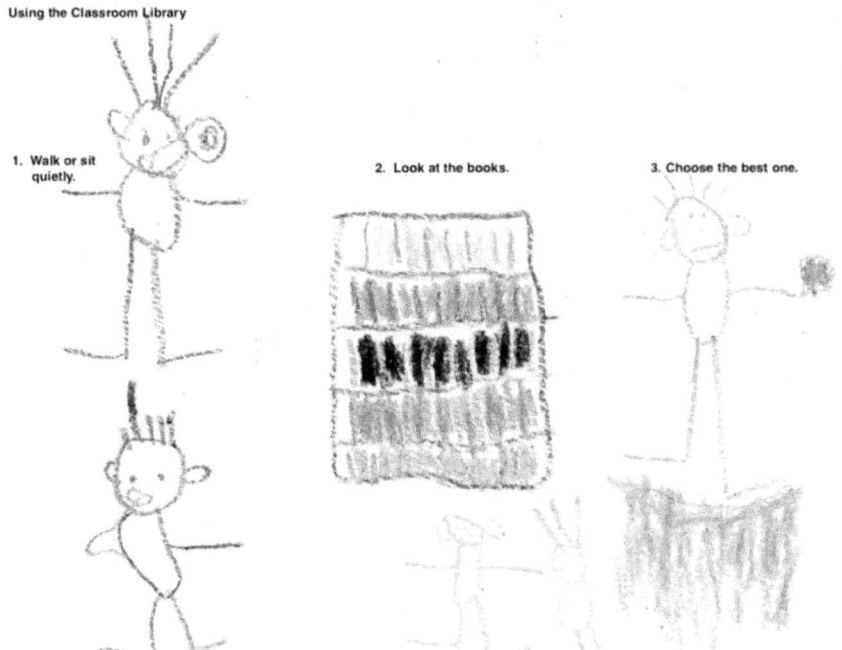

Figure 2.5   Example of a child-created library usage chart for a Pre-K classroom

- L: learn about books
- I: ignite your passion for reading
- B: browse collections
- R: read, read, read
- A: arrange your book collection and area
- R: read, read, read some more
- Y: yearn to put books in the hands of children each day!

Principle 3

Avoid the One-Size-Fits-All Approach

Becoming the best literacy teacher you can be requires a belief that all children learn differently, that one size does not fit all. It compels a commitment to teaching all children individually. It may even mean that you let go of some long-running practices that have dominated classrooms for years.

TALK ABOUT AVOIDING THE ONE-SIZE-FITS-ALL APPROACH

Think about this conversation between Haley, a teacher, and Kendall, a literacy coach in figure 3.1. What feels familiar about this conversation? What surprises you?

Avoiding one-size-fits-all teaching requires you to start with daily, authentic assessment. Letter learning is no different, as Kendall explains to Haley. This allows teaching based on the needs of each child.

In principle 3, you will learn how to avoid generalized practices. You will be introduced to the importance of individualizing instruction, assessing children through multiple measures, and using observation as a driving force for teaching literacy in early childhood classrooms. Before you begin to read, reflect on the list of things to avoid below (figure 3.2). Have you seen teachers failing to avoid any of them?

⚠ **Avoid thinking of children as the same simply because they are the same age**

Just like no single snowflake is the same, no child is the same. Children come to us with different life experiences, learning needs, and interests. They are intricate.

Haley: My Letter of the Week lessons have not been going very well. This week, some students did not want to sit and focus when I introduced the letter 'G.'

Kendall: Hmm…were you teaching the letter to the whole class?

Haley: Yes, students repeated the letter and sound while I showed them pictures of words that begin with the letter. Some children seemed bored; they looked around and didn't participate.

Kendall: Remember when you administered the Marie Clay Observation Task for Letter Identification; did you notice how some of your students already had knowledge of the letter 'G,' its sounds, and words that start with 'G'?

Haley: I did, but I was under the impression that I was teaching based on team planning where we emphasize particular letters each week.

Kendall: Consider what you can share with your team. Clay tells us to "find out which letters the child knows and then seek a fast route to his learning the others" (2005, p. 85). We know that some letters and sounds are easier to learn than others; it makes sense that our teaching focuses on what individual children still need to know about letters and sounds. They may be bored because they already know the information that you were trying to teach them.

Figure 3.1 A little talk about avoiding one size fits all

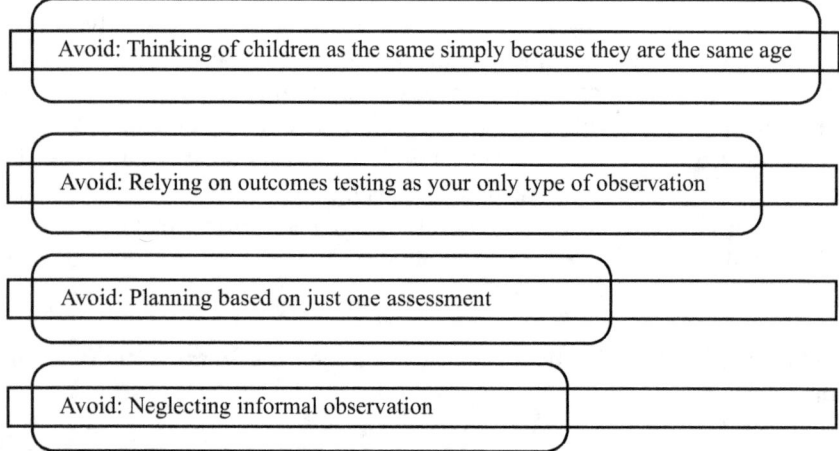

Figure 3.2 List to promote thinking about practices that we can omit in order to promote more individualized instruction

When we see the snow falling, each flake looks identical; they all fall together to create a landscape that looks uniform. But, when we put two snowflakes under a magnifying glass, they have unique and different characteristics. So, if we know that all children are so different, why do we assume we can teach them all the same way?

Consider two five-year-olds. They are both forty-two inches tall and weigh about thirty-eight pounds. They both like to ride bikes and play with Legos. They both love the book *Ada Twist, Scientist* by Andrea Beaty. They both like simple games, can follow most rules, and like spending time with other kids.

On the surface, they seem the same, and while we know that psychologists like Piaget (1952) and Erikson (1956) have identified developmental levels based on age groups, as teachers we still have to dig deeper to identify the unique needs of each child. Not one of them will truly be equal, so we cannot teach them the same way.

While there have been programs developed that calculate individual needs of children (Connor, Morrison, Schatschneider, Underwood, & Crowe, 2009), it is really through interacting that you make significant decisions about what is best for each child. Watching and learning from the children allows you to take the lead from the child and not from a computer algorithm. If you are not making the time to watch and really observe, it is time to re-evaluate your practices.

Have you read the poem "Me I Am" by Jack Prelutsky (1983)? The first stanza announces, "No Me I Am has been before and none will ever be." Each year, you will teach different *Me I Am's*. You will have never seen them before, and you will never see them again. Think about it that way. Children may have some things in common, but none are exactly the same.

You *must* adjust your teaching to that idea. It is not easy, but it is vital. When you master individualization, you will find your greatest success. Imagine how your children will thrive. This principle 3 will show you ways to assess each child so that you are aware of individual needs, and subsequent principles will help you learn how to use your assessment results to teach to those individual needs.

⚠ Avoid relying on national or state testing as your only type of observation

Classroom-based observational assessment is different from what most identify as *testing*. Tests that are given at the national, state, or district level are most often tests of outcomes. "State and national tests provide the public and policymakers with a snapshot of how children are doing in reading and other areas. But these kinds of tests fail to provide teachers with the kind of diagnostic information (i.e., actionable data) needed to plan effective instruction" (Reutzel & Cooter, 2019, p. 405).

What happens with these types of tests in literacy is that we assess children in August and use that data for grouping, like in high-, middle-, and low-reading groups, or we assess them in May and determine end-of-the-year reading success or failure based on a one-shot performance. This is a poor way to make instructional recommendations for children. Often these types of tests do not give enough information to teachers. They:

- Provide no item analyses to show the actual questions asked and the actual answer the child provided
- Abandon detailed individual results in favor of group results related to gender, race, special populations, and so on
- Focus on what children cannot do

While these tests give an overview of performance, could you use this information to assist you in individualizing your literacy instruction? The short answer is *no*; you cannot.

These national-, state-, and district-level tests are not villains, however. They do have a place in the classroom. It is how we react to these tests that could be bad. If we don't spend hours on test preparation, and we use the results as a general evaluation of our teaching, that is a good thing. It is when we begin to do more test preparation with children than actual teaching of the content and when we use the results as diagnoses for individuals that the tests become villains.

When we fall into this trap, we focus on the piece of paper with the test results instead of on the child herself. What types of assessments do you think teachers can add to balance these large-scale tests that would help them better meet the needs of individual students? Keep reading to find out.

⚠ Avoid planning based on just one assessment

There are many reliable and valid literacy assessments for screening, diagnosing, and monitoring individual children (Reutzel & Cooter, 2019). Some of these feel more formal, more like tests. They assess a range of literacy skills from concepts about print to reading comprehension. A majority focus on very early literacy skills, like phonological awareness and letter naming; these are frequently used in early childhood classrooms.

These assessments are usually quick and easy to administer, systematic, and provide information about the link between early literacy skills and later reading success. They give us individualized results and, for example, tell us whether or not an individual child has mastered rhyme production or letter names for visually similar letters like *b*, *d*, and *p*.

Reliably developing these assessments may be much easier than developing literacy assessment for more complex skills like emergent book reading and academic vocabulary; because of that, we have much research about phonological awareness and letter identification (Snow & Oh, 2011). As a result, many schools rely on the plethora of assessments and studies that exist to create curriculum for early literacy that is heavily focused on these two areas. While phonological awareness and letter identification are very important, we caution you to remember to assess children for the many other literacy skills needed for success as well.

Just because one assessment is quick, easy, and readily available does not mean it should be the sole indicator of what a child knows. You have to dig deeper to find assessments that provide the most meaningful connections about the gamut of literacy skills that children possess. Remember, assessing naturally and regularly through multiple means is essential to developing teacher plans that best meet the needs of every child. No one assessment can tell us everything we need to know about a child's literacy strengths and needs.

Some inexpensive and notably reliable and valid formal assessments that teachers can learn to easily administer include the *Flynt/Cooter Comprehensive Reading Inventory-2 Assessment for K-12 Reading Skills in English & Spanish* (Cooter, Flynt, & Cooter, 2014) and *An Observation Survey of Early Literacy Achievement* (Clay, 2005). Teachers can purchase both for under $100 and have a battery of assessments on hand, including concepts about print, phonological awareness, letter identification, decoding, fluency, comprehension, and writing. These provide a great start to help you avoid relying on one assessment to individualize instruction. In addition to these, there is another vital assessment that is easily administered every day: informal observation.

⚠ Avoid neglecting informal observation

Observation is an authentic way to daily gather the most information about individual children. Snow and Oh (2011) indicate that testing should not be privileged over observational measures and that observation is "a highly informative supplement to test results" (p. 379). It is a natural part of the regular classroom routine. As an observer, you are an active collector of the pieces that put together the puzzle of who each child is as a literacy learner.

So, why wait? Start putting the puzzle pieces together today. Learn about your children; *observe*. Observations reveal both strengths and weaknesses. Think about how schools use computer programs to calculate reading levels. These do not give much detail about actual reading behaviors; only watching a child read and taking careful observational notes can provide the valuable pieces to the puzzle that inform instruction for that child.

Try this to determine how effectively you can collect small puzzle pieces. Without actually looking, think about what your eyes look like (color, shape, etc.). You have had years to observe what they look like, right? So, this should be easy. Write down what you know about how they look. Now, go and look in a mirror. Take the time to really investigate. How did you do? Did you notice anything that you have never seen before?

We look at children all day long, but we truly do not see the intricate pieces until we learn *how* to observe—to really look harder than just a glance. Sometimes what we think we remember from those glances is not what is actually there. Just like with your eyes, when we really spend time in deep observation, we find that there is much more detail for us to discover about each child.

Remember to always LOOK when observing children. Use this process as a guide:

1. *L*ead exploration of literacy, using play and talk.
2. *O*bserve with purpose, continuing to be a participant who facilitates.
3. *O*rganize what you see through documentation, avoiding judgment.
4. *K*now what the documentation means, interpreting carefully.

While this is written in a linear fashion, this process is more interwoven. The teacher may observe, then lead, then observe, then document, then lead more, and so on. It might be a messy process; embrace that it is a *process*.

LEARN TO BE AN EFFECTIVE OBSERVER

In observation, the teacher does not need to be this silent *watcher*, sitting in a corner who waits for a child to display some level of literacy learning. Observation can be interactive and can be used to build relationships with children. Teachers simply need to find a balance between leading and observing.

Below, we discuss each piece of LOOK and use a dramatic play example to show how a teacher can apply LOOK to observation. The skills observed in the scenario are adapted from Pre-K guidelines in our state (Texas) and accurately represent what four-year-old children might do when playing together.

Lead Exploration of Literacy, Using Play and Talk

Observation may seem easy and unplanned to those looking in, but in reality, it takes time to think about the best ways to gather information. You may have to:

- Anticipate and acquire materials needed
- Build centers that promote literacy
- Investigate developmentally appropriate literacy skills found in your standards
- Choose literacy skills to observe
- Think about how you might lead during the observation

This planning lets you know when you should step in to trigger engagement with literacy skills and when you should step back and let the engagement unfold on its own. Once you have investigated literacy standards for your children and developed play centers rich with opportunities for literacy learning (more information to come about that in Principles 4 and 6), you are ready to observe and lead exploration.

Socializing through play, as part of a daily routine, is an opportune time for you, as the teacher, to encourage children to explore literacy in natural ways. While some play is impromptu in early childhood classrooms, other play should be thoughtfully planned. In coordination with teaching based on your standards, set up play areas that extend standard-based skills.

For example, in a restaurant-based sociodramatic play center, a teacher may provide menus from local restaurants, pads and pencils for writing, aprons, dishes, plastic food, cookware, tables, chairs, and more. She purposefully sets up an environment where children can comfortably play and explore literacy. Then, she can become a deliberate observer who facilitates explorations.

Imagine the sociodramatic play center described above where three children are playing. Sometimes the children invite the teacher to play, but if they do not, she should always ask before joining. The teacher becomes a part of the play by interacting and using dialogue. In the example below, consider how Ms. Zhou is leading exploration of literacy, specifically for emergent reading, writing, and oral language.

José, David, and Julia prepare The Rocket, their restaurant, for visitors. They clean the stove, sink, and table with towels. They place matching plates and cups on the table. They set out menus and talk about how to prepare lunch. Ms. Zhou comes into The Rocket and says, "I'm so hungry. Are you open for business?" José excitedly answers, "Yes!" David leads Ms. Zhou to the table and says, "Please sit here."

David hands Ms. Zhou the menu and asks what she wants to eat. Ms. Zhou notices that David does not have any paper with him to take the order, so she asks, "You might want to write my order down." David responds, "Oh yes, I forgot" and takes out his pad of paper to write. Ms. Zhou tells him that she wants chicken fingers with fries, so David writes, "CKN FNGRS AND FRS" and takes the paper to Julia and José. Julia says, "Chicken fingers with fries, coming up!"

Think about how Ms. Zhou led the children to engage with literacy. She asked questions. She never told them what to do; she encouraged them to think about how to use literacy. Ms. Zhou responded to what the children were doing naturally and purposefully led them through play. She did not go too far in her leading, but she went just far enough. How do you think Ms. Zhou facilitated emergent literacy?

Observe with Purpose, Continuing to Be a Participant Who Facilitates

Julia places David's order on a piece of string hanging on the wall by the stove. José follows the text with his finger and says, "Chicken fingers with French fries." Julia asks José how to make chicken fingers, and both look very puzzled. Ms. Zhou reminds them that there is a recipe box near the refrigerator that might help.

Julia pulls out a recipe card with a picture of chicken, points to the words, and begins to read aloud, moving her finger across the card. "Get chicken. Put crunchy stuff on it. Cook it in the pan for one hour." José pipes in: "One hour? That's too long. Are you sure that's what it says?" Julia rereads and says, "Yes, one hour!" Julia starts preparing the chicken, and José says, "I'll make the fries because I have seen them make fries at Whataburger®." While the children work out the issues with the food, Ms. Zhou quickly makes notes about the dialog and literacy behaviors.

Meanwhile, David returns to Ms. Zhou's table and asks, "Do you want something to drink." "I will have sweet tea, thank you," Ms. Zhou says. He grabs the order form again and quickly writes, "SWT T." José puts the food on the plate and says, "It's ready." They hand Ms. Zhou the order and watch expectantly.

During this part of the observation, what do you think Ms. Zhou saw in terms of reading, writing, and oral language? Was she able to lead them to engage in the skills that she wanted to observe? Julia wrote the order. David read the recipe. José used critical thinking and asked for clarification. And, all three children used language to propel the play. Ms. Zhou had opportunities to observe emergent reading, writing, and oral language, yet she never controlled the play. She was simply a participant observer. Now, what do you think Ms. Zhou should do with what she observed?

Organize What You See through Documentation, Avoiding Judgment

Rejoining the scenario, Ms. Zhou tastes the food and tells José and Julia that they are wonderful cooks. While David and José clean the dishes, Julia greets a new customer. Ms. Zhou takes this as her cue to leave the center, which gives her time to add to her documentation that she recorded in the moment. What would you include in the documentation? Remember, Ms. Zhou pre-planned to look for specific literacy skills.

Use a Checklist

Documentation takes on many forms. Before observing, research various forms of documentation. Choose the documentation style that best meets

Table 3.1 This example depicts skills related to literacy, and it shows how you can quickly mark a skill as mastery, developing, or didn't observe

	Julia	David	José
Understands symbols convey meaning	M	M	M
Conveys left to right directionality	M	M	M
Uses conventional spelling	X	D	X
Responds appropriately	M	M	M
Takes turns in conversation	M	M	M
Asks/Responds to questions	M	M	M

Key: M=mastery; D=developing; X=didn't observe

your needs. For instance, if you are new to observation, you may start with a checklist. It offers a very quick glance at categories of skills and is easy to use. A checklist is a bit more limiting because you cannot include every literacy skill that you would ever want to see, but it is a very good place to start. Table 3.1 illustrates a portion of what a checklist would look like if we apply it to the example above with Julia, David, and José.

Table 3.1 gives us an idea of what Julia, David, and José can do in terms of oral language, writing, and reading. In the sociodramatic play, David writes an order, and Julia and José read and interpret the order. As you can see, all three children show evidence of mastery of the skill related to understanding that symbols convey meaning. Similarly, all three children respond appropriately, take turns when talking to each other, and ask or respond to questions. The checklist shows mastery of these oral language skills as well.

Julia's and José's finger pointing show that they are reading from left to right. David's print shows that he is ordering letters from left to right. The checklist shows evidence of mastering directionality. It should be noted, however, that in order to identify true mastery, Ms. Zhou will want to observe those skills over multiple occasions.

David was the only child who wrote anything, so only David could be evaluated for use of conventional spelling. Because David is missing vowel sounds but has correctly matched consonant sounds to letters, he is still developing his use of conventional spelling.

Try an Anecdotal Checklist

When you become more comfortable with observation and with the literacy skills you want to see, you may want to use an anecdotal checklist. This allows you to take your own notes yet still provides the scaffold of the list of skills. Writing out your own anecdotes does take a bit more time, but it provides more specifics about the skills being observed. The anecdotal checklist is a great transition to practice with more detailed observational notes.

Table 3.2   The example depicts skills related to literacy and shows how checklists can also contain anecdotes

	Julia	David	José
Understands symbols convey meaning	Reads recipe; rereads to confirm information	Writes order; accurately captures the food order chicken fingers, fries, and sweet tea	Reads order; interprets food order and adds an additional meaningful word "French"
Conveys left to right directionality	Reads recipe; uses finger pointing from left to right	Writes "CKN . . ." Consonants represent the order of sounds, from left to right	Reads order; uses finger pointing from left to right
Uses conventional spelling	Did not observe	"CKN FNGRS, etc. . . ."; approximates spelling	Did not observe
Responds appropriately	"Chicken fingers with fries, coming up!" Uses restaurant lingo	"Please sit here." Uses social conventions of language (pragmatics)	"Yes!" Responds to question
Takes turns in conversation	Doesn't talk over others; listens, waits for turn to speak	Doesn't talk over others; listens, waits for turn to speak	Doesn't talk over others; listens, waits for turn to speak
Asks/responds to questions	"Yes, one hour!" Responds with additional detail but not complete sentences	"Oh yes, I forgot." Responds with complete sentence	"Are you sure that is what it says?" Asks questions to find out information

Table 3.2 gives more detail about each of Julia's, David's, and José's literacy skills. The checklist (table 3.1) shows that all three children mastered understanding that symbols convey meaning, responding appropriately, taking turns when talking to each other, and asking or responding to questions. However, with the anecdotal checklist (table 3.2), we can see the specifics.

For example, under the skill of *responds appropriately*, Julia uses a response that requires schema for restaurant jargon. David's response shows his knowledge of social conventions of language. José, however, has a simple response with no additional details added. Being able to write anecdotes on the checklist provides this insight into each child's individual knowledge.

In addition, instead of just knowing that David conveys directionality and understands symbols (table 3.1), the anecdotal checklist (table 3.2) now specifies that his skills are related to writing, while Julia's and José's skills with directionality and meaning are related to reading. Also of importance is that we can now see how David is developing conventional spelling; he has command of the use of letter and sound correspondence for consonants only. He is still lacking vowel awareness in his spelling. All are important details that can impact the way that we instruct David.

Take Anecdotal Notes

When you write notes on an anecdotal checklist, you can make important distinctions. As you become proficient with the anecdotal checklist, you internalize the developmental skills your children need. You will no longer be dependent on having a list of skills in front of you for all observations. Perhaps, then, you will want to try an even more comprehensive way to document your observations.

Anecdotal notes are a narrative record of what you observe. You write both what the child is doing and details of what you see in terms of the skills that you have internalized. It is important to capture dialogue and specifics about behaviors. Anecdotal notes take time and require that you have much schema for what you need to see within the observation. They can be organized on sticky notes, index cards, digital notebooks, and so on. Figure 3.3 shows anecdotal notes for the dramatic play example with Julia, David, and José.

In figure 3.3, you can easily see the skills represented in both the checklist and the anecdotal checklist, but now the anecdotal notes provide a glimpse into even more literacy behaviors. Anecdotal notes provide a wider range of skills than a checklist because the abundance of literacy skills that children might exhibit would not fit onto one checklist. The anecdotal checklist confines the observer to only the notes that fit into the box.

For example, take a look back at the two types of checklists (tables 3.1 and 3.2). What do you see in the anecdotal notes (figure 3.3) that is missing from the checklist in terms of Julia's reading behaviors? Julia used pictures to derive meaning while reading when she relied on the picture of the chicken to find the right recipe card. This is an important part of beginning reading, using pictures to assist in decoding.

Now, investigate the observations about sentence structure use in the anecdotal notes. Do you see these skills represented in the checklists? The checklist did not have any skills related to the use of sentence structure in oral language or writing. Yet, Julia and David use simple sentences, and José uses a complex sentence when talking. The observation in the anecdotal notes gives us much more information about the sophisticated oral language skills of the children.

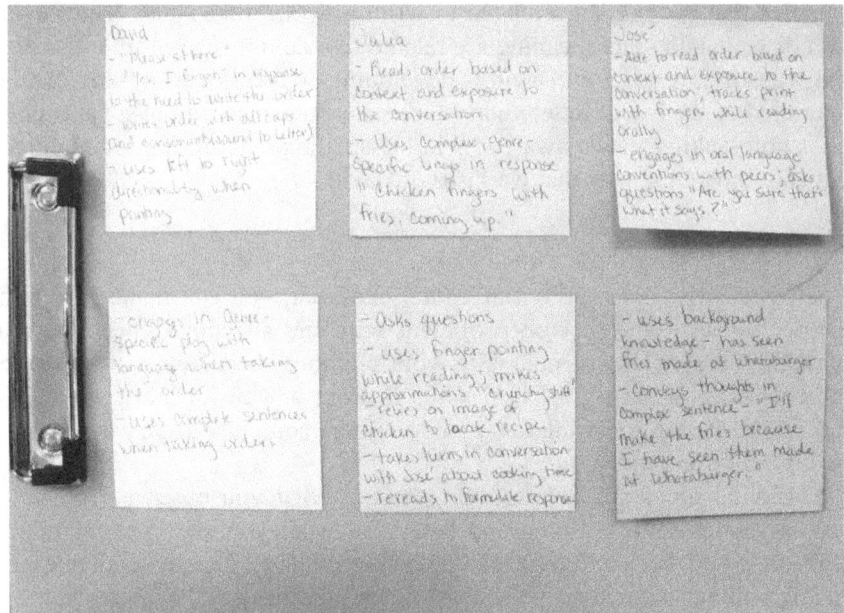

Figure 3.3 This example depicts skills related to literacy, and it shows how the teacher has to have a knowledge of skills to note

Checklists and anecdotal notes are just some of many types of observational documentation. Choose the format that best meets your needs, and do not feel bound to one particular format. As you can see, each of those described here provides different levels of information and requires different commitments of time and background knowledge.

Consider taking paper checklists and anecdotal notes into a digital format if you are comfortable with technology; some digital platforms may make data collection and analysis easier for you. Here are a few ideas to explore:

- Use digital note-taking software like Microsoft OneNote or Stickies to record anecdotal records (smart pens and touchscreens even allow you to handwrite digitally instead of type).
- Use iPads or other small devices to record or photograph learning to enhance anecdotal records or update checklists later (be sure to have the appropriate permission/release).
- Investigate for-purchase software and apps like Kaymbu (portfolio tool), iAuditor (checklist generator tool), Evidence for Learning (comprehensive observational assessment tool), Learning Genie (portfolio and assessment tool), and so on.

No matter which form of observational documentation you use, you will ultimately need to interpret the information so that you can individualize instruction.

Know What the Documentation Means, Interpreting Carefully

After observing students, you should review the documentation to look for both a child's strengths and his or her areas for improvement. When you teach based on these two things, you will ensure the greatest potential for growth. However, be careful about drawing too many conclusions from one assessment. You need data from multiple assessments in order to plan instruction.

For example, the anecdotal notes in figure 3.2 did not note that José uses directionality. If Ms. Zhou only uses that one observation, she may think that José has not learned to attend to directionality. However, this conclusion should not be drawn without more evidence.

Instead, be sure to observe over time and in varied situations where children are both in and out of the action of play (Jablon, Dombro, & Dichtelmiller, 2011). Just like tests, you don't want to use just one assessment as an indicator of a child's knowledge. Just because you didn't see the skill in one observation does not mean that the child cannot accomplish the skill. Table 3.3 gives an example of how Ms. Zhou might use multiple assessments to make instructional recommendations for Julia.

Through fun and authentic activities, Julia can be encouraged in a variety of ways: to attend to the idea that print carries meaning, to learn how authors use print in texts, and to learn new vocabulary in her favorite books. Read alouds and alongside reading experiences are great opportunities for allowing Julia to explore these concepts about print and to begin to practice using these in her approximations toward reading and writing. Of course, we would never expect Julia to master these new skills during the first interaction with text. Careful consideration must be taken to ensure that the learning is natural and never forced.

Maria Solis, (figure 3.4) an early childhood principal, shares how assessment impacts her school. How does she encourage the teachers to authentically collect and use assessment data in order to avoid one-size-fits-all teaching?

Observation can be one of the most powerful assessments tools if the time and care is taken to LOOK. In the example, the observation was done in a natural setting; the children were simply playing together in a dramatic center. It is important to point out how much we could tell about the three children

Table 3.3 Data from three assessments and individualized recommendations for Julia

Julia	Observation	Cooter/Flynt/Cooter & Concepts about Print Tests	Writing Sample
Oral Language	Interpretation: Uses simple sentences while speaking and understands conventions of oral language (waiting to speak, listening, responding on task, etc.)	No assessment	No assessment
Reading	Interpretation: Makes approximations toward reading by using pictures and schema to assist with meaning-making; tracks print with fingers, moving from left to right	Assessment results: Knows front and back of book, where to begin reading, to start with print, difference between pictures and words, difference between letters and words	No assessment
Writing	No observation	No assessment	Sample results: Wrote "HR PTR" and included an illustration of a child on a broom in response to favorite book

Individualized Recommendations:
- Provide more opportunity for Julia to engage in speaking with peers and adults through play and response to classroom activities.
- Use favorite texts to exemplify complete thoughts/sentences and higher-level vocabulary, and encourage her to use that vocabulary in her sociodramatic play conversations and writing.
- During one-to-one read alouds and alongside reading, guide Julia into using the images and first letter(s) of words to begin to attend to print and make meaning of individual words.
- Encourage Julia to extend her thoughts and begin to use lowercase letters in her own writing.

in this one play scenario because we took the time to broadly evaluate each child's development. Look at all of the data you have.

Assessment practices in many preschools, kindergartens, and primary grade programs have become mismatched to children's cultures or languages, ages, or developmental capacities. As with curriculum, assessment instruments often focus on a limited range of skills, causing teachers to narrow their curriculum

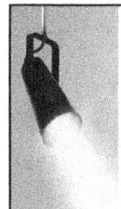 

Spotlight on Practice

Maria Solis

Principal

I think anything a child creates can be considered assessment. It's important for it to be authentic. It's about getting to know the child, having conversations, and listening to the children. You can gather data in the cafeteria, watch children in centers, and even observe when they are engaged in conflict. You have to have an intentional eye to look for opportunities for assessment.

Since literacy connects to everything, you can find opportunities there. The classroom should be oozing with literacy. There should be a library where reading and writing are integrated. The library should be the place where everyone wants to go. Children should be immersed in read alouds and given a chance to talk and write. Observation is about what teachers can see during interactions.

Years ago assessment meant something different to teachers. Now, teachers are more in tune in with the purpose of assessment, how it drives instruction, and how to adjust it to meet the needs of students. Teachers know it should be useful and purposeful. They know more about avoiding a one-size-fits-all approach.

At my school, we've made it more about individual children. Teachers have a portfolio box where they collect children's work. Our teachers also keep anecdotal records in binders with sections that make it easy to share individual information with parents. We value the input that parents can give us.

This year we even eliminated meet the teacher; instead, it's about meeting the parents. At my school, we invite parents to talk about their children. We start with something simple like, "Tell me about how you decided to give your child his/her name?" Assessment starts with knowing the child and knowing the families. It's understanding the whole child, not just the academics.

Figure 3.4 Spotlight on practice: Maria Solis, principal

and teaching practices (that is, to "teach to the test"), especially when the stakes are high. (NAEYC & NAECS-SDE, 2003, p. 4)

Assessment is the key to resolving the mismatch and avoiding the one-size-fits-all approach; observation is the most important part of that. It really is that simple. Make this a priority. When we become preoccupied with the daily classroom minutia (paperwork, high-stakes results, overemphasis of one skill over all of the others), we lose sight of what is foundationally important in children's development, and we cannot be the best teachers we can be. Dedicate yourself to LOOK, and you will truly see the instructional needs of children.

Principle 4

Link Development and Play to Literacy Learning

As a teacher of young children, it is important to set the groundwork for growing and learning. Play provides an opportunity for children to learn in a developmentally appropriate way and form a strong foundation for literacy development. Read about what research has to say about play and literacy (table 4.1).

While these studies represent a sampling of those that are experimentally designed, researchers have found similar positive impacts of play on literacy with other research designs as well (Korat, Bahar, & Snapir, 2002/2003; Lysaker, Wheat, & Benson 2010; Neuman & Roskos, 1997; and more). "What could be more academic than developing ideas from experiences? Yet, most schools separate students' hands from their minds, minimize exploration, and narrow risk taking to simple interactions with a piece of paper or a computer" (Washor & Mojkowski, 2006/2007).

TALK ABOUT PLAY

Have you ever wondered about the importance of play or why children need to play? Have you ever watched children playing and been surprised by the things they say? Listen to Mrs. Fuller, a principal, and Mr. Jackson, a kindergarten teacher, discuss play in an early childhood classroom (figure 4.1).

Teachers, like Mr. Jackson, who have an awareness of developmentally appropriate practice (DAP) understand how to create classroom activities that account for how children learn (individually, socially, culturally). Teachers who embed play into their daily routine help build a developmentally appropriate classroom that serves as a comfortable place for children to explore literacy. In this principle you will learn what DAP means, how play is a springboard

Table 4.1 The chart displays empirical studies that support dramatic play as rigorous activity that can enhance critical literacy skill development

Literacy Skills Significantly Changed through Dramatic Play	Study 1	Study 2	Study 3	Study 4
Phonemic Awareness	✓			
Phonics	✓			
Vocabulary	✓			
Oral Reading	✓			
Environmental Print Word Reading				✓
Emergent to Conventional Reading (browsing/book handling, pretend reading, oral and silent reading)		✓		
Storytelling Format/Genre	✓			✓
Storytelling Structures (plot, characters, setting, etc.)	✓			
Oral Narrative Comprehension Length, Complexity, and Coherency			✓	
Emergent to Conventional Writing (drawing, tracing/copying, dictating, scribbling/writing/typing)				✓
Story Writing (including invented form writing)				✓
Paper Handling Behaviors (sorting, shuffling, scanning)				✓

Notes:

Study 1: Cavanaugh, Clemence, Teale, Rule, and Montgomery (2017). This experimental, counterbalanced study involved two classes of kindergarten students divided into four groups. The control play was teacher-created, rote sorting activities for phonemic awareness and phonics. The experimental play asked the children to create their own games for practicing target phonemic awareness and phonics skills. There was a statistically positive effect on the DIBELS assessment for students after completing the experimental play. Additional literacy skills were observed for the experimental play that were not present during controlled play.

Study 2: Vukelich (1994). This experimental study included fifty-six kindergarten participants randomly assigned to three groups: thematic play with related environmental print and an adult play participant, thematic play with related environmental print and no adult participant, and thematic play with no direct infusion of environmental print or adult participant. The researchers examined field notes/video and conducted pre- and post-testing with Clay's Concepts About Print test, reading environmental print in context, and reading environmental print out of context. The researchers found statistically significant positive results for reading environmental print both in and out of context for the group that participated in thematic play with related environmental print and adult play participation.

Study 3: Baumer, Ferholt, and Lecusay (2005). In this fourteen-week study, two groups of kindergarten and first-grade children were read *The Lion, the Witch, and the Wardrobe* by C. S. Lewis. The experimental group engaged in adult-led dramatization and play in response to reading. The control group engaged in adult-led activities like reading, writing, and discussion in response but no dramatic play. All participants were given pre- and post-tests for narrative competence and length, which included narrative production to show understanding of story, sequence of actions, and causal motivation related to the book. At post-testing, the experimental group had a significant change in narrative comprehension length, coherence, and complexity.

Study 4: Roskos, Morrow, and Rand (1991). This experimental study with 170 preschool and kindergarten children analyzed children's literacy behaviors across four groups: play groups with adult guidance where literacy tools had been added, play groups with adult guidance where literacy tools were related to a theme, play groups where literacy tools were related to the theme but there was no adult guidance, and traditional curriculum with play centers where no modifications were made. The first statistical analysis conducted after a treatment period showed significantly more engagement with the literacy behaviors (emergent to conventional examples of reading, writing, and paper handling) for the two groups with adult involvement in relation to the two groups without adult involvement.

Principal Fuller: Mr. Jackson, tell me about your classroom; it seems unorganized and noisy.

Mr. Jackson: Well, it's actually very organized. Take a look at the Publishing Company learning area. The kids are studying rhyme. "Jack and Jill" is written on chart paper. There are rhyming books from read alouds, props for dramatizing, and pictures for rhyme matching and games. The center has publishing schedules and paper, writing tools, and materials for publishing.

Principal Fuller: To me, it looks like they're just using those materials to play.

Mr. Jackson: You are right; they are playing. But, do you see what LaTrece is doing? She is using the pointer to track the rhyme print as Will is saying the rhyme with her. Keep watching.

Principal Fuller: OK, I see that.

Mr. Jackson: Now, they are acting out the rhyme. Did you hear how Will pointed out that Jill and Hill rhyme? And, now he just noticed that Jill and Hill rhyme with his name? After they explore and play, they will begin publishing their own rhyme books.

Principal Fuller: But, I'm worried that playing won't give us high results on benchmarks.

Mr. Jackson: Children learn through play and can work beyond what I normally expect. I'm observing and collecting data daily. I'm confident that they will do well on any benchmark.

Figure 4.1 A little talk about learning through play

for developmentally appropriate learning in learning areas, and ways to root literacy instruction in play. Principle 4 will help you see why you should:

⚠ **Avoid eliminating play from your curriculum**

⚠ **Avoid restricting and controlling play**

⚠ **Avoid limiting the link between play and literacy**

Before reading further, quickly sketch (drawings, words, etc.) your ideas about literacy learning that takes place during developmentally appropriate play. Use your sketch as you read. Make changes as you learn more about development and play.

GET TO KNOW DAP

Some people think they have an idea of what DAP is, but what they think may not always be accurate. Because DAP encompasses multiple components, often teachers believe that their practices are developmentally appropriate when they are, in actuality, missing one of the most important pieces. DAP, according to the National Association for the Education of Young Children (NAEYC, 2009), is complex and requires a balance of what we know from theory/research and what we know about the:

- Group: milestones associated with an age group
- Individual: strengths and weaknesses of each child
- Context: classroom environments that promote intentional, individualized learning

A teacher who practices DAP knows how to teach the whole child, attending to each of those parts. Ask yourself these questions about every lesson or activity that you do with young children to ensure you are using developmentally appropriate teaching (Copple & Bredekamp, 2009):

- Does this activity align with what I know about the physical, cognitive, and social/emotional milestones for this age group?
- Does this activity address the strengths and weaknesses of this individual child?
- Does this activity fit within the context of an intentional, culturally responsive classroom?

If the answer to any of these questions is *no*, revise or rethink the activity. "Effective early childhood professionals draw on all the principles of child development and learning . . ., as well as the knowledge base on effective practices, and they apply the information in their practice" (NAEYC, 2009, p. 16).

Recognize Developmentally Appropriate Emergent Literacy Practices

In terms of literacy instruction, Almy's 1949 pivotal study spurred a belief that children are always at various stages of emerging as readers and writers, despite age. Correlational analyses between mental age and learning experiences (play-based or formal) and reading accomplishment showed that mental age did not determine success. It was learning experiences that addressed where a child was developmentally in literacy emergence that determined success. In other words, success was related to developmentally appropriate practice.

"Today, research stressing the role of social interaction and the importance of the child's prior experiences and knowledge has led to preschool instructional practices that eschew the drill and practice of isolated skills and instead emphasize a range of 'hands-on/minds-on' developmentally appropriate activities that foster both children's social-emotional and academic competencies" (Teale, Brown Hoffman, Whittingham, & Paciga, 2018, p. 188).

Teale and Sulzby's 1986 review of work in the field of early literacy learning became a book that has now been in print for over thirty years. Their publication was groundbreaking in terms of how we think about child-centered, authentic literacy learning experiences. This work "became a manifesto for emergent literacy" (Teale, Brown Hoffman, Whittingham, & Paciga, 2018, p. 190).

Prior to these works, children were not considered ready to read until they had mastered letter names/sounds and decoding skills. There was no consideration for the differences in individual children or classroom contexts. In other words, DAP was not a consideration for literacy education.

Now, we know that children can begin reading and writing before mastery of those basic skills. With emergent literacy, on average, children of a certain age tend to display specific literacy behaviors. However, it is important that we also pay attention to the literacy strengths and weaknesses of each child. We consider what we know about literacy learning for all, what we know about a child as an individual literacy learner, and what we can do in the classroom context to enhance emergent literacy growth. This is DAP; it is what builds balanced literacy.

The current political climate with push-down academics might lead you to believe that a focus on DAP would be at the expense of a focus on academics. However, this is not true. DAP activities and instruction can be academically rigorous (Copple & Bredekamp, 2009). How better to strengthen the literacy skills of a young child than through a focus on individual needs that is rooted in theory and research? DAP allows for this; it serves as the bricks that provide a strong academic foundation.

What may surprise you is that play can be the avenue that leads to rigorous literacy learning for all children. Go back to your sketched notes that you made earlier; can you add to your prior knowledge of DAP? What elements would have to be included in play to represent DAP? Add or amend your notes based upon your thinking.

DEFINE THE GOOD FOUR-LETTER WORD: P-L-A-Y

Play is a simple four-letter word. However, it is not easy to define. It is fluid because it changes based upon the players and the context. So, play is very complicated.

Children are naturally curious and use play to make sense of the world around them. They use schema to create play scenes and scenarios that help them explore and learn through manipulation of materials. Play challenges thinking and is some of the hardest work a child will ever perform.

Consider Teacher-Directed Play

Some early childhood teachers narrow play in their classrooms to fun, cute activities that generate a product. These activities are often focused on explicit instruction. For example, *Catalina Magdalena Hoopensteiner Wallendiner Hogan Logan Bogan Was Her Name* by Tedd Arnold is a great way to get children thinking about rhyme and phoneme substitution. It is a fun option for playing with names. You can model how rhyme and substitution work by letting the children help you create your own funny name, for example, Amelia Bedilia Miller Stiller Hewitt Bewitt Pewitt.

The work with rhyme and substitution can then continue in a learning area where children play with names. While at the learning area, they come up with their own new name and audio record it on the iPad. This allows them to play back the audio repeatedly and hear the way the rhyme and substitution work. Children work together to develop a scene where they introduce their funny name. Finally, they video record themselves with the iPad so others can watch the scene later.

During this play, children are having fun while working on two important literacy skills, but the teacher has already elected what the product will be (e.g., the video that exemplifies rhyme and substitution). The children are directly focusing on the two skills but have limited control over certain parts of the play (e.g., the practice is name-based only, the scene is narrowed to introduction, and they make a video product). The play doesn't have room to grow and expand, which would broaden the literacy skills that the children might encounter.

Sometimes this type of narrowly focused play that utilizes explicit instruction has its place in the classroom. However, imagine if this play were sociodramatic, thematic, and the children were given more control over their play. Where would the play go? What could children learn about literacy?

Think about how Isabel McHan talks about play in the Spotlight on practice (figure 4.2).

What did you learn about how Isabel views play? How is it different from the teacher-directed play discussed previously? One of the highest forms of play occurs when children are engaged with peers.

Sociodramatic play encourages children to interact with others and encompasses a wide variety of academic skills in a setting that allows for talk, creativity, and role playing. It is child centered, as opposed to activity centered. It has been consistently linked to academic success (Baumer, Ferholt, & Lecusay, 2005; Cavanaugh, Clemence, Teale, Rule, & Montgomery, 2017; Morrow & Rand, 1991; Roskos & Christie, 2013; Vukelich, 1994; and more).

Spotlight on Practice

Isabel McHan

Pre-kindergarten Teacher

I teach prekidergarten in one of the largest urban school districts in the United States, and children play in my classroom each day. I have a firm belief in the use of play in teaching; however, I did not start with this belief. I used to restrict imagination and creativity by telling children where to go and what to do in the classroom.

The play in my classroom is now child led; it is about meeting children's needs. It's about honoring everything they do. I have shifted my thinking from the classroom being *my* classroom to the children running the classroom. My role is as a facilitator and a model.

When the children begin playing in centers, they start with parallel play, often playing on their own and not acknowledging each other. Sometimes I bring in another teacher to model vocabulary to promote play with each other. As the year goes on, the children's conversations with one another become more complex; they begin solving problems, coming up with their own ideas, and taking it beyond what I thought they would. Different centers are implemented each year, depending on the interests of the children.

I introduce play centers with something that is familiar. For example, I might give the children time to explore a center with blocks. Then, I can introduce *The Three Billy Goats Gruff* and encourage them to try to build a bridge from the story. I might say, "You can do this now, so, what can you do next?" Based on what they want to do next, I find materials so that the children can build and expand the center over time. The children have ownership of it.

Play comes naturally to children and can be rigorous. Rigor happens when children dig deeper into the content while engaging in intentional and meaningful play. When we take play away, we take away an opportunity for children to learn. Play-based centers allow for this learning and give children the time to practice social-emotional, abstract, and critical thinking skills. Teachers in every grade level need to find out what play means for their students and incorporate it!

Figure 4.2   Spotlight on practice: Isabel McHan, prekindergarten teacher

Isabel understands the benefits of sociodramatic play in her classroom, and research certainly provides ample evidence that sociodramatic play experiences are a crucial component of a child's early learning years. The question is how do we practically apply this research.

DISCOVER iZONES

We want to revolutionize your way of thinking about sociodramatic play with a new term: *iZone (Interest Zone of Natural Education)*. iZones are *not* traditional teacher-led center areas. They are interest areas within your classroom that promote choice, sociodramatic learning, and the natural evolution of skills. iZones are designed with an intention to encourage children to interact with materials, the teacher, and other children.

You may be thinking that this doesn't sound any different from traditional learning centers. Well, let's update your thinking. iZones are designed with the help of the children. They are not prepackaged or preplanned by a company or by the teacher. iZones are created with intention and are based upon a skill(s) children need or express an interest in knowing more about.

The materials in sociodramatic iZones are dynamic and offer a multitude of avenues to explore. Encouraging children to confront certain literacy skills can be accomplished with strategic placement of materials and modeling. However, children still direct their own play.

Consider Sociodramatic Play in an iZone

While the children should have options, you may have particular literacy skills you want the children to practice. For example, if you are focusing an observation on rhyme and phoneme substitution, you can set the stage to see those skills in a sociodramatic iZone.

After reading aloud *Catalina Magdalena Hoopensteiner Wallendiner Hogan Logan Bogan Was Her Name*, you might offer a short minilesson about rhyme and phoneme substitution and work with the children to create their own anchor chart of fun names. The anchor chart can be placed in a farm iZone (because the children are interested in farms), and you might write on the bottom of the chart, "Can you give your farm animal a fun name?" This prompt will encourage children to continue to practice rhyme and phoneme substitution when they visit the iZone.

Consider what else might be included in your farm iZone. Next to the chart is a basket of farm animals in all shapes and sizes (plastic or stuffed cows, pigs, horses, chickens, sheep, llamas, camels, etc.), a stethoscope, plastic food, pen/pencils, lab coats or scrubs, hats, and so on. There is plenty of paper (manila, chart, white copy, lined, etc.). There are books, magazines, and other texts for reading about both fictional and real farms. Children are encouraged to explore and use even more levels of literacy. Some things that you might see children doing in this iZone are:

- Continuing to practice with phoneme substitution by naming other items on the farm; e.g., Chicken Licken, Piglet Wiglet.
- Keeping track of feeding schedules for the animals and creating shopping lists for buying food.
- Documenting animal behaviors and health issues.
- Reading developmentally appropriate books about animals, farms, plants, and so on.
- Drawing and labeling plans for pens, barns, and so on.
- Creating books with stories about the animals.
- Researching a Farmer's Almanac, farming magazines, and weather reports to determine when to plant crops.
- Representing how to plant crops, to track growth, and so on, using graphs.
- Completing medical documents and prescriptions as the farm veterinarian.

During this thematic, sociodramatic play, children investigate literacy in their own way. Do you see how much more they can practice in this example compared to the first example where the teacher directed the play? In an iZone where children engage in sociodramatic play, they extend their play through oral language, draw on knowledge from prior experiences, read, write, investigate, and so on. They regulate the course of the play, and through the process of *playing* with skills, they sustain learning in a way that greatly benefits even the youngest child.

What does this mean for you? Think about the characteristics that might make sociodramatic iZones the most successful. Take a look at figure 4.3, which shows thematically linked learning areas in Isabel McHan's prekindergarten classroom. What things could children do to explore and use literacy? Add your ideas to the sketch that you started at the beginning of principle 4.

APPLY THE IMPORTANT COMPONENTS OF EFFECTIVE PLAY TO YOUR IZONE

Rand and Morrow (2018) reviewed pivotal studies about play's positive effect on literacy and confirmed the need for planning and facilitation. So, don't assume that you are not an important part of the play equation simply because children will direct the play.

Plan with Children

Planning for playful learning in an iZone requires that we know the individual needs of children. We also need to make sure that our literacy activities are

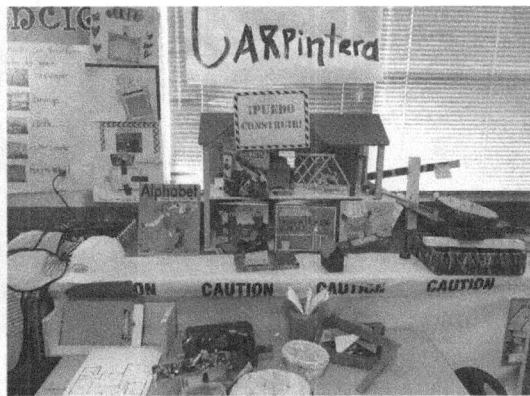

Figure 4.3 The construction and carpentry learning areas in Isabel McHan's PK classroom

broad, instead of narrowly focusing on reading and writing only. Creating areas for this type of play takes a high level of planning, as you can see in the following steps:

1. Use observational assessment, and gather information on individual students in your class and the class as a whole.
2. Consider inviting the children into the planning; talk to them about their interests; conduct a brief survey to ask them what they would like to learn more about.
3. Select the theme for the sociodramatic iZone; let the children's interests guide the selection of the theme.
4. Determine standards that can be addressed in the iZone.
5. Explore thematic materials; read and talk with the children about the iZone's theme, exposing them to authentic materials so they see how people use literacy, collaborate, and work within the theme's context; let the children suggest materials to explore or take part in the construction of the area.

This planning time is actually setting a course for how the children will explore literacy in the learning area. For example, in the farm iZone, children may not know how a farmer uses a Farmer's Almanac or farming magazines to plan crops. Through teacher-guided investigation with these materials, the children learn what farming really looks like and will be able to imitate that through their play. Your role is to intentionally guide the creation of the iZone so that the children learn academic skills.

64   Principle 4

Isabel McHan did just that when her children created a learning area related to NASA. They built the area with McHan and guided her in selecting the appropriate materials and literacy learning. Figure 4.4 shows what this looked like after her intentional planning with the children.

Address the Literacy Needs of Each Child

Everything has a purpose if we teach with intentionality. In terms of play, intentionality involves careful consideration of the environment, observational assessments, standards, DAP, and literacy activities. Because of intentionality, we know the children and their needs very well, so we can create iZones that are conducive to practicing certain literacy skills. Of course, an

Figure 4.4   NASA learning area in Isabel McHan's PK classroom

intentional teacher will also leave room for the children to explore and learn in more complex ways.

In the Neuman and Roskos (1990) pivotal study, intentionality with the creation of learning areas for play led children to engage in "literacy-related behaviors even though there was no evidence of this kind of role related literacy play before the intervention" (Rand & Morrow, 2018, p. 244). When children have time to explore purposefully crafted learning areas, they "create practice sessions that are customized to individual needs, interests, and abilities" (Pickett, 2005, p. 272). You will often see children practicing surprisingly complex skills in iZones.

One last thing to consider with intentionality is not allowing your own biases to overshadow the needs of your children. When creating these iZones, you will have schema for materials and scenarios that go with the thematic area that the children selected, but that schema may not match what your children have in those situations. For instance, instead of just having horses, chickens, and cattle for your farm area, you will also want to include farm animals from other countries, like oxen, camel, and alpaca.

Facilitate Playful Learning

Rand and Morrow (2018) suggest that specific types of "adult guidance and scaffolding during play can improve literacy learning" (p. 252). Vygotsky's (1978a) work with scaffolding and the zone of proximal development helps us to understand why facilitation is so important. He explains, "Children can imitate a variety of actions that go well beyond the limits of their own capabilities. Using imitation, children are capable of doing much more in collective activity or under the guidance of adults" (p. 88).

Through facilitation, you assume a flexible, supportive, and "maieutic" (based on Socratic inquiry) role in advancing children's play situations (Morrow & Schickedanz, 2006). iZones are designed so that you become a learner as well, a learner who is immersed in a classroom that is fluid and dedicated to meeting the needs of the children. In addition, you are an observer, documenting mastery of skills and making plans for reteaching or individualizing instruction for students who either did not address the skills during play or had misconceptions or struggles with those skills.

Your role as a teacher-facilitator could also include *leading*, *playing*, *extending*, and *directing/redirecting* (Morrow & Schickedanz, 2006). *Extending*, *leading*, and *playing* will come naturally and happen frequently during purposeful play. For example, if children name their farm animals with a funny name, you can *extend* that by asking, "What will you name the barn, the pond, or your farm?" Maybe, a child says one of the farm animals is sick. You can then *lead* the child to write down the symptoms, helping her to match initial letter/sound correspondence in her words. You can offer to play the veterinarian and then write a prescription. Your *play* serves as a model for specific writing behaviors.

Sometimes you will also have to *direct/redirect* purposeful play. Maybe, during the play, the child writes his animal name, "mig pig," but you have already taught the skill of capitalizing the first letter of names. You can *redirect* the child to the specific anchor chart that was created to look at examples of proper nouns written during language experience writing. Be mindful of directing/redirecting children too often. Use judgment, and redirect only when specifically necessary.

Although facilitators can assume various roles during play, *leading*, *extending*, and *playing* are more effective ways to assist learning (Morrow & Schickedanz, 2006). "Active scaffolding of imaginative play is needed in early childhood settings if children are to develop the sustained, mature dramatic play that contributes significantly to their self-regulation and other cognitive, linguistic, social, and emotional benefits" (NAEYC, 2009, p. 15).

BRIDGE PLAY AND ACADEMIC LITERACY WITH RIGOR

Combining academic rigor with DAP may seem like a juxtaposition of extremes. "However, rigor and developmentally appropriate practice do not have to exist in opposite realms; they can peacefully coexist in the same space with best practices that serve the needs and interests of young children" (Brown, Smith Feger, & Mowry, 2015, p. 63). Because play is a developmentally appropriate practice, it stands to reason that we can create play environments that peacefully coexist with rigorous academics. But, what is it that would make that play more academically rigorous than other forms of instruction focused on academic skills?

Sociodramatic iZones offer children robust opportunities to challenge thinking. It is this blend of authentic practice within an environment that begs for inquiry and exploration that pushes the rigor. Children must think critically about the choices they make in play situations that have connections to how academic skills are used in the real world. "We must try to reconcile the need for formal instruction with the potential that play settings generate in children and early learning" (Rand & Morrow, 2018, p. 251). Play and rigor can align.

Look for Rigor in Examples of Play

Consider what might happen with academics in a whole-group circle time scenario. A teacher engages the children in choral reading of the welcome message, uses a pointer to help children attend to print while singing a rhyming song, calls on volunteers to help read the calendar, and writes the date on the board.

While these are certainly great skills to practice, think about how the practice is happening. Is it rigorous? Does it require critical thinking? Are the children applying the learning in a way that we would in the real world?

Now, how could those same skills be enhanced in a rigorous way through a sociodramatic iZone? In the farm iZone, Sidney is playing the farmer today. Sidney walks into the barn, finds the calendar, and notices that today is Tuesday. He picks up the animal care journal and reads Monday's entry about Mig Pig's visit to the veterinarian. Under the entry, Sidney records Tuesday's date and writes a new entry about Mig Pig feeling better. Think about what is happening in Sidney's play. Is it rigorous? Does it require critical thinking? Is Sidney applying the learning in a way that we would in the real world?

In the whole-group circle time, children are sitting with eyes focused on the teacher. The activities are teacher led with a limited number of children engaging, and when they are engaging, their responses follow a closely prescribed expectation. Where is the evidence of critical thinking when you only call on a few students to answer and when you limit the types of interaction with literacy? In addition, there is no connection to how we use literacy in real life. Normally, we do not write the date out on a board in our homes. When we do, though, it is for a purpose, like adding an appointment to the calendar and writing the date on a letter or email.

In the farm iZone, Sidney has the opportunity to use the calendar in the barn, and he has to critically evaluate when and how a farmer actually uses dates. The farm area encourages Sidney to have a more advanced response to the calendar. He connects his response to prior learning experiences in meaningful ways. The literacy skills he uses are much more advanced than simply writing the date on a board or chorally reading a morning message. He is actively controlling his learning and engaging with it in a more rigorous way.

Rigorous, developmentally appropriate play is a blend of what we know is appropriate best practice and academic skills that are often highlighted in standards for learning. It depends heavily on the children engaging in inquiry, critical thinking, and application. Rigorous play requires careful attention. In order for rigorous play to be successful, include these components in your intentional planning and facilitation:

- Scaffolding and supporting play
- Providing multiple and integrated play opportunities for each academic skill

- Connecting schema to playful learning, connecting that learning across domains (physical, cognitive, social/emotional) and content
- Encouraging collaborative discourse and play
- Graduating the learning of academic skills within the play so that they slowly build across time
- Observing play experiences carefully and using that observation to facilitate play (Brown, Smith Feger, & Mowry, 2015).

If you are still not convinced that play can offer rigorous learning opportunities that address skills/standards, look back at table 4.1.

Sociodramatic play, especially that in which the adult *extends*, *leads*, and *plays*, has the potential to allow children to explore, practice, and grow literacy skills in a rigorous way. iZones provide room for imagination, and actions (like literacy-related behaviors) come out of imagination. "Action in the imaginative sphere, in an imaginary situation, the creation of voluntary intentions, and the formation of real-life plans and volitional motives-all appear in play and make it the highest level of preschool development" (Vygotsky, 1978a, p. 102).

Vygotsky's theoretical framework for play highlights the importance of social learning and creating opportunities for social mediation. "Play provides a risk-free context for children to practice and experiment with language and literacy skills and to apply general knowledge" (Nell, Drew, & Bush, 2013, p. 20). Since literacy is a key to all learning, then what better way to introduce anything but through developmentally appropriate, sociodramatic play in iZones?

Before leaving principle 4, go back to your sketch that you started at the beginning of this principle. Have you made some revisions? Are there more revisions to be made? What other information can you add? Hang on to your modified sketch because you will be able to use it as a guide for better understanding principle 6.

Principle 5

Share Daily, Delightful Read Alouds

The delightful read aloud has to be a part of your daily interaction with children. "It is an early-life intervention that seems to be beneficial for the rest of [children's] lives" (Kalb & van Ours, 2014, p. 21). It is one of "the most powerful literacy events for motivating listeners to emulate adults' love of reading" (Sanacore, 2006, p. 34). Reading aloud to children daily helps to develop lifelong readers, and that is what we should want for all of the children we teach. So,

⚠ **Avoid Risking a Child's Love of Reading!**

Read aloud to your children every day, and make those read alouds delightful experiences.

TALK ABOUT READING ALOUD

Figure 5.1 highlights two teachers sharing their experience with reading aloud. Think about the elements of the read aloud that would make it engaging for children.

Choosing the *just right* book can make a simple read aloud experience turn into something magical and beyond the ordinary. Teachers who read aloud see the wonder and excitement in the eyes of the children who are listening.

In principle 5, you will learn about daily, delightful read alouds, which provide natural interactions and induce critical conversations between a reader and child(ren). So, when we say *read aloud*, that is what we mean. In principle 7, we will show you how to use a shared read aloud experience to teach emergent skills, which is something quite different. For now, let's focus on why it is important to read aloud, the cycle of reading aloud, how to create

Stephen: Yesterday, I read *Don't Let the Pigeon Stay Up Late*, and the kids had so much fun.

Amanda: Oh, I love that one! My students love it when they get to tell the pigeon, "No!"

Stephen: Yes, Juan yelled the loudest, and you know he's usually the quietest person in class.

Amanda: I would've loved to see that. I bet the kids love it when you play the part of the pigeon, begging, crying, and stomping your feet.

Stephen: Yep, they laugh along with me, but you know, it took a lot of practice to get right.

Amanda: Yeah, but reading those books over and over to practice is so worth it.

Stephen: I agree. The kids giggle and giggle when the pigeon yells, "I'M NOT TIRED!" They can really relate to that.

Amanda: That's because they've been in the same place as the pigeon. I think they like the power of playing the part of a parent during the read aloud.

Stephen: It's really amazing how it all comes together when we select the *just right* book to read aloud.

Figure 5.1 A little talk about reading aloud

an effective read aloud with the *just right* book, and the enjoyment of hearing a story read aloud.

Bring Joy to Read Alouds

What does it mean to read aloud? In educational settings, the read aloud is often mistakenly used only to teach a specific emergent skill and never focused simply on enjoyment and meaning. However, think about what reading aloud looks like at home with children; it is joyful and focused on the meaning of texts. You want your read aloud to mimic this. Your read alouds should convey the passion you have for seeing a book come to life.

As we have learned from Louise Rosenblatt (1994), it's the reader who breathes life into meaning by connecting to texts that have been skillfully crafted by an author. Your role while reading aloud is to show children this interaction (or *poem*, according to Rosenblatt) between a reader and text; it's an interaction that is super important for future reading experiences, including comprehension and reading motivation.

In order to make meaning, readers think about the text, question why events happen, make predictions about those events, and connect with them on a personal level. This is what makes literature and nonfiction texts enjoyable to read.

Talking about the interactions with a text can make reading aloud even more enjoyable. So, a read aloud should be a natural experience where the reader and children talk together about what is happening; they construct meaning together. They enjoy the text together. Fifth-grade teacher Ghida Hijazi practices daily, delightful read alouds in her classroom (see figure 5.2). Her spotlight story shows just how to bring joy to reading aloud.

Make Read Alouds Impactful for Learning

As early as 1882, researchers were writing about the importance of reading aloud (Christenson, 2016), and it is still being studied today (Ledger & Merga, 2018). There is no doubt that reading aloud is something we should be doing.

From their review of literature, Ledger and Merga (2018) highlight research that has shown the importance of reading aloud in general. It positively impacts:

- Literacy level development
- Reading intervention effectiveness
- Print convention acquisition
- Comprehension, vocabulary, and cognitive development
- Motivation and reading frequency
- Receptive skills
- Language demands in other curricular areas
- The prevention of aliteracy in later life

But, what does research say about daily, delightful read alouds specifically? There are two key points to remember.

1. Read aloud daily. The more this happens, the greater the benefits for students.
2. Read alouds should include critical conversation. The key is hearing the book, thinking, and talking deeply about what it means.

Too often, this type of read aloud is skipped because it is seen as "educational fluff" or not as important as shared or guided reading experiences that are used to teach letter learning, decoding, or other emergent skills. Research has shown us that daily, delightful read alouds are invaluable and important enough to warrant our attention *every day*. Figure 5.3 shows two major issues when it comes to reading aloud:

Spotlight on Practice

Ghida Hijazi

Fifth-Grade Teacher

I read aloud at the beginning of our literacy block every day! It helps build relationships and is a good way to create a bond between me and the children. The read aloud is a time in the day when I can have conversations with the children that go way beyond just the standards. I can teach them something in the read aloud and then use the minilesson later to show them what they learned. You really can teach your minilesson *before* you actually teach the minilesson.

Selecting the book for the read aloud takes time. I look at the weekly standards and choose books and questions that would support those. When the children choose books to read independently, they choose lots of fiction. I read mostly non-fiction. I want to show them that non-fiction can be read for pleasure too. The books chosen relate to real life issues; children don't get enough of that.

Every day I get three or so children who are eager to show me books they want read aloud. The children always say, "You have to read this book to us!" They pick books that I would pick. They pick books with life lessons. This amazes me!

We have a pre-reading discussion, a think aloud, and a "thinking job" where they think while I am reading. Children turn and talk about three times during the read aloud, and we do an after-reading discussion. If I don't plan the questions I will ask, I find that the level of questions is just so easy. It takes practice, and I still struggle with that.

At the beginning of the year, my read alouds are seven minutes maximum. The children aren't able to answer higher-order questions because they are not making connections yet and need time to practice. They also need to build stamina for longer read alouds. Later in the year, the children:

- Make more connections with the book
- Answer higher-order questions
- Come up with life lessons
- Want to read longer

If a read aloud takes longer than the 15-20 minutes that I plan, I sometimes have to break up books over a few days, but the children always beg me to keep reading.

Reading every day educates us in so many ways. I'm excited when I see the children in class modeling the read aloud process! When reading to other children, they read just like I do.

Figure 5.2 Spotlight on practice: Ghida Hijazi, fifth-grade teacher

- Parents and teachers simply are not reading to children as often as they want and need. This tragic issue may continue to get worse as society becomes more and more preoccupied with digital devices that isolate us from time with children.

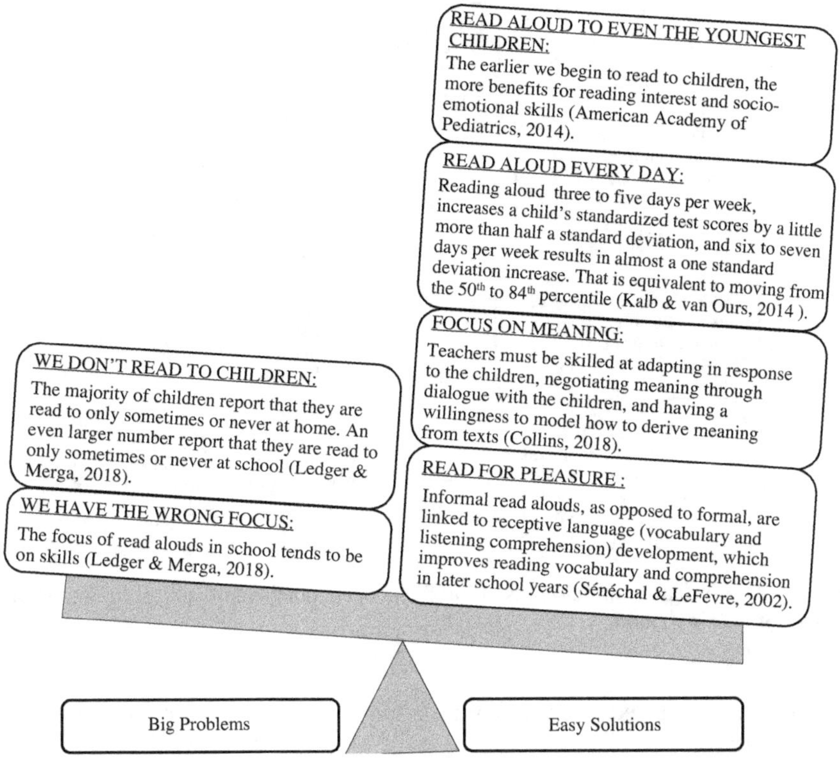

Share Daily, Delightful Read Alouds

READ ALOUD TO EVEN THE YOUNGEST CHILDREN:
The earlier we begin to read to children, the more benefits for reading interest and socio-emotional skills (American Academy of Pediatrics, 2014).

READ ALOUD EVERY DAY:
Reading aloud three to five days per week, increases a child's standardized test scores by a little more than half a standard deviation, and six to seven days per week results in almost a one standard deviation increase. That is equivalent to moving from the 50th to 84th percentile (Kalb & van Ours, 2014).

FOCUS ON MEANING:
Teachers must be skilled at adapting in response to the children, negotiating meaning through dialogue with the children, and having a willingness to model how to derive meaning from texts (Collins, 2018).

WE DON'T READ TO CHILDREN:
The majority of children report that they are read to only sometimes or never at home. An even larger number report that they are read to only sometimes or never at school (Ledger & Merga, 2018).

WE HAVE THE WRONG FOCUS:
The focus of read alouds in school tends to be on skills (Ledger & Merga, 2018).

READ FOR PLEASURE:
Informal read alouds, as opposed to formal, are linked to receptive language (vocabulary and listening comprehension) development, which improves reading vocabulary and comprehension in later school years (Sénéchal & LeFevre, 2002).

Big Problems | Easy Solutions

Figure 5.3 Scale showing easy solutions that will outweigh the problems we currently face with reading aloud

- When read alouds are actually done in schools, they tend to be very scripted and focused on teaching a basic skill, which is likely to continue as a precedent because there is so much focus on test performance. These types of read alouds are needed but should *not* take the place of reading for pleasure.

VIEW READING ALOUD AS A CONTINUOUS CYCLE

Reading aloud sounds simple, but it's not. It requires careful consideration and planning to be effective. Take some time to consider the read aloud graphic (figure 5.4). Think about your experiences with reading aloud, either someone reading to you or you reading to children.

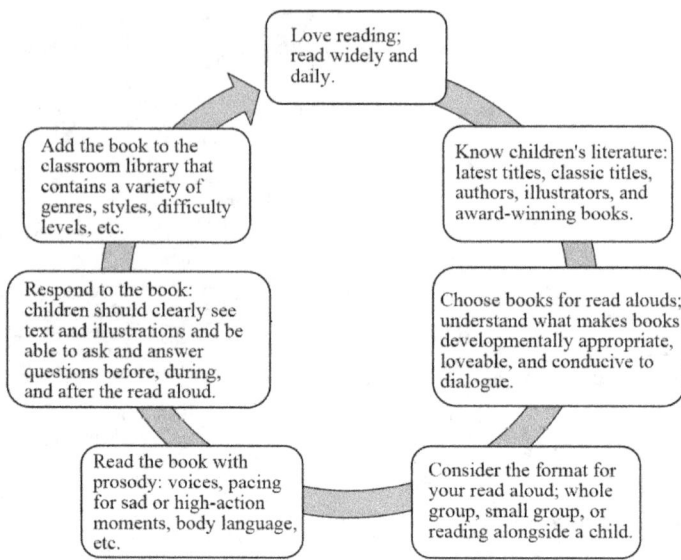

Figure 5.4 Circular graphic representing the process teachers of young children should follow for reading aloud

- How have your experiences with reading aloud evoked a passion and love for reading?
- How do your experiences fit within the graphic?
- Consider why the graphic is circular.
- What would happen if one of the pieces was missing?

The graphic represents the cycle of reading aloud to children. Notice how it begins with reading on a daily basis, knowing what children's literature is available, and choosing books for reading aloud that are appropriate and engaging. Then, it moves to determining who you will be reading the book with, practicing how the book should be read aloud, and encouraging children to respond to books. It ends with building a classroom library that offers various texts for children to experience. The process is cyclical and begins again where it ends.

Choose *Just Right* Books

When it comes to reading aloud, children's interests are plentiful and dynamic, giving you plenty of options for selecting *just right* books. Sometimes a child will request favorite titles, a book based on a topic, or a picture book with intriguing images. You can read these requested books for the child's enjoyment.

Don't be surprised when children ask for their favorite book to be read over and over; this is a normal part of developing lifelong readers. The requests and repeated favorites help build children's literacy confidence and reading skills in a DAP way. Even though you may be weary of hearing the same stories over and over, the children are really working in a deep and meaningful way when they repeat the familiar words or "chorus" of a book as they read along with you.

For instance, with two to three years old, Sandra Boynton books are a popular choice for reading repeatedly. One such book is *Barnyard Dance*. Children become immersed in the rhyme and rhythm of the book as they pretend to be different animals, singing and dancing along with the story.

Because children do have read aloud requests, you won't necessarily have much time to prepare. This is why it is important for you to read widely in the world of children's literature and for you to know your classroom library very well. You must know the titles and authors in your library. This will help you to be prepared to read aloud a child's request in an engaging manner and promote important dialogue about the book. The only way to do this is to immerse yourself in children's literature; that is why reading widely is the first piece of the read aloud cycle.

Daily read alouds can also be based on your consideration of the needs of children. Select books with a particular topic or conversation in mind. The read aloud should "engage [children] in text-to-life and life-to-text talk, prompt children to talk, and use child-involved analytical talk in discussions about stories" (Collins, 2018, p. 223). So, when picking that *just right* book for the read aloud, look for books that have a developed vocabulary and storyline. This allows the reader to get lost in the text and ultimately want to tell someone about what he or she is feeling and hearing. The book selected should motivate children to want to know more because it peaks interest.

You may want to expose children to a well-known author, specific vocabulary, or a literary concept. For example, a kindergarten teacher may choose a book from the Ramona Quimby series by Beverly Cleary in order to encourage engagement with the whole series. Don't be intimidated about reading aloud chapter books with young children. Early chapter books introduce children to texts that they eventually will be able to read and critically evaluate alone. Children learn to visualize the story, ask questions about what is happening, and build larger vocabulary and reading stamina for more complex books, all the while developing listening comprehension.

Here are some guidelines for you to consider when selecting developmentally appropriate books for young children (Children's Book Council, 1995; Hoffman, Teale, & Yokota, 2015; Koralek, 2003).

- Infants: Fun language and illustrations; bright colors and simple text (rhyme and repetition); concepts that are familiar like animals, babies, daily routines, familiar objects. Examples include books like *Pat the Bunny* by Dorothy Kunhardt or *Ten Little Fingers and Ten Little Toes* by Mem Fox.
- Toddlers: Fun language and illustrations; themes that allow for simple questions and discussion and a combination of predictable to more complex text that introduces new vocabulary and more challenging plot structures; personal connections like feelings, people, places, events; concepts like shape and color. Examples include books like *Bear Snores On* by Karma Wilson and *Five Little Monkeys Jumping on the Bed* by Eileen Christelow.
- Pre-K and K: More complex language and text; longer picture books, chapter books, and books they will be able to "reread" on their own later; more detailed, refined illustrations; themes that allow for deeper questions, connections, predictions and lots of discussion. *Dragons Love Tacos* by Adam Rubin and *Love* by Matt de la Peña are excellent examples.
- Primary: Advanced language and vocabulary; concepts and themes that extend beyond what the child has experienced; opportunity for critical thinking, discussion, and extended research. *Junkyard Wonders* by Patricia Polacco and *The Poppy Lady: Moina Belle Michael and Her Tribute to Veterans* by Barbara Elizabeth Walsh are just a few of many examples.

In addition to selecting books that are developmentally appropriate, it is important to have a variety of books in your classroom that would be of interest to your students and also address critical literacy skills. The following list introduces books that build on these qualities (table 5.1). This list is only a small part of many, many authors and books that are available.

This is certainly not an exhaustive list. We want to encourage you to commit to getting to know books beyond this list. You can probably think of some of your favorites to add to the list right now. Be sure to spend time in your library and at bookstores finding more great books to include. When you have knowledge of children's literature and strategically make time for impromptu and planned read alouds each day, you are paving a firm reading path for children.

Scaffold Read Alouds

When you read to children, you become a model for them. You provide cognitive support as you facilitate the read aloud and the conversation that surrounds it. Picture scaffolding on the outside of a building. It works to support

Table 5.1 Included are some favorites of young children that evoke delightful dialogue and critical literacy skills

Author	Book	Why?
Authors with Books in a Series		
Mo Willems	*Knuffle Bunny*	Relatable, interactive stories; fun illustrations
Jonathan London	*Froggy's Sleepover*	Fun, relatable stories and repeated dialogue that encourage read along; colorful illustrations
Mercer Mayer	*Just Go to Bed*	Relatable stories and simple text; colorful illustrations
Jane Yolen and Mark Teague	*How Do Dinosaurs Get Well Soon?*	Fun, relatable stories with rhyme and simple text; colorful illustrations
David Shannon	*David Gets in Trouble*	Fun, relatable stories and simple text; colorful illustrations
Eric Lipwin	*Pete the Cat: I Love My White Shoes*	Fun, relatable stories and simple text; colorful illustrations
Doreen Cronin	*Click Clack Moo: Cows That Type*	Fun stories with imbedded lessons; colorful illustrations
Aaron Blabey	*Pig the Pug*	Fun stories with imbedded lessons and engaging illustrations
Favorite Fiction Authors		
Eric Carle	*The Very Quiet Cricket, From Head to Toe,* and more	Simple stories with predictable text that encourage read along; colorful illustrations
Kevin Henkes	*Kitten's First Full Moon, Waiting, Lilly's Purple Plastic Purse,* and more	Developed *heart* stories with imbedded life lessons; sophisticated illustrations
Audrey and Don Wood	*The Napping House; Quick as a Cricket; The Little Mouse, The Red Ripe Strawberry, and The Big Hungry Bear;* and more	Simples stories with rhyme and predictable text that encourage read along; colorful illustrations
Bill Martin Jr.	*Polar Bear, Polar Bear, What Do You Hear?, Chicka Chicka Boom Boom,* and more	Simple stories with rhyme and predictable text that encourage read along; colorful illustrations
Laura Numeroff	*If You Give a Dog a Donut, If You Give a Pig a Pancake,* and more	Circular stories with predictable text that encourage read along; colorful illustrations

Continued

Table 5.1 (Continued)

Author	Book	Why?
Dr. Seuss	*The ABC Book, The Foot Book*, and more	Rhyme, rhythm, and colorful illustrations
Iza Trapani	*Twinkle, Twinkle, Little Star; The Itsy Bitsy Spider; How Much Is that Doggie in the Window?*; and more	Song-based rhyme and rhythm with engaging illustrations
David Wiesner	*Flotsam, The Three Pigs*, and more	Well-developed wordless stories that prompt questions and inferences; sophisticated illustrations
Keith Baker	*Big Fat Hen, Hickory Dickory Dock, No Two Alike*, and more	Song-based rhyme and rhythm with colorful illustrations
Margaret Wise Brown	*Goodnight Moon, Big Red Barn, The Runaway Bunny*, and more	Relatable stories and colorful illustrations
Keith Faulkner	*The Wide-Mouthed Frog* and more	Engineered, fun illustrations and imbedded life lessons
Favorite Nonfiction Books		
Melissa Sweet	*Some Writer! The Story of E.B. White*	Interesting narrative true story; unique format including primary source images; relatable link to *Charlotte's Web*; sophisticated illustrations
Maira Kalman	*Fireboat: The Heroic Adventures of the John J. Harvey*	Simple factual story to build knowledge, colorful illustrations
Jeanette Winter	*My Name Is Georgia*	Simple narrative true story to build background knowledge, simple illustrations
Susan L. Roth and Cindy Trumbore	*The Mangrove Tree: Planting Trees to Feed Families*	Beautiful combination of poetry, narrative nonfiction, and exposition; beautiful illustrations; moving story to promote philanthropy and change

and hold up people or equipment. That is exactly what you are doing for children when you scaffold them as they reach high for meaning in the text.

Vygotsky (1978b) indicated that children benefit from the knowledge of a more experienced learner. Because your role in the read aloud is the experienced reader, you must:

- Know the developmental needs of children and carefully select *just right* books and lead *just right* conversations so that learning takes place within the zone of proximal development (not too hard but just hard enough to move a child forward in learning)
- Value high-support strategies over low-support strategies. Support their reading comprehension as you ask questions, vocabulary development by "gushing" over interesting and unique words, and oral language development and listening comprehension as you talk, enunciate words, and add prosody to the read aloud (Pentimonti & Justice, 2010; Verenikina, 2008)

As the reader, it is your role to responsibly scaffold in order to facilitate an experience that is appropriate for each child, taking into account age, individual need, and culture.

Create Engaging Read Alouds

Read alouds should be comfortable and exciting. They should mimic an enjoyable experience and provide meaningful interaction. If you had positive "at-home" reading experiences as a child, think about how natural and comforting those experiences were. If you did not have parents who read to you, imagine what the ideal read aloud would look like with a parent and a young child.

Envision a child choosing a book and running to a parent, sibling, or caregiver and asking for that book to be read. The child jumps into the person's lap and snuggles close to listen to the book. While it is not always possible to have children in your lap, the children should be close to you and the text. The idea is that everyone feel comfortable enough to lose themselves in the read aloud.

Young children like to move. So, do not be surprised if they move around during a read aloud. This does not mean that the children are not focused on the text being read. Forcing all children to sit still, instead of allowing movement, will often result in disruption to the authentic aspect of the read aloud.

Don't ever force a read aloud for the very young. Children need time to build listening and reading stamina. Infants and toddlers may only focus on what is being read aloud for a matter of seconds, so choosing short and very engaging texts might be best. But, also know that you may have some infants and toddlers who can focus on much longer read aloud experiences. *No two children are the same.* Know your students and give them what they need individually in read aloud experiences.

Whatever you do, just know that building the stamina to sit and listen to a read aloud from an author such as Patricia Polacco or Chris Van Allsburg will require time. Take baby steps, be patient, pay attention to cues your children are giving you, and never make reading aloud feel like a chore or punishment.

In addition to accepting some movement during a read aloud, you should think about how to invite and guide conversation before, during, and after the read aloud. Ledger and Merga (2018) found that some children do not like a lot of interruptions during the read aloud. Be prepared to redirect talk that is not related to the story or to ask children to wait for the answers to some questions, especially if you know that subsequent pages will reveal information to help them arrive at answers on their own. Validate their thoughts with a quick "That's a good question; let's wait to see if it gets answered later." Come back to the question later.

While some dialogue between the reader and children needs to happen during the read aloud, much of it can take place before and after (Dickinson & Smith, 1994). Remember, read alouds teach children about literacy, but most importantly, they should be fun. So, find the balance between the perfect amount of dialogue and the quiet time to listen to the story.

At the very beginning of the school year and using reminders throughout, work with the children to set some guidelines for read alouds. Do a brief interview by asking children what makes a good read aloud for them. Ask:

- How do you like to sit in order to best enjoy the read aloud?
- What do you think other children should be doing?
- Do you like to ask questions during the read aloud?
- Do you like it when other children ask questions or have comments?

Based on these important conversations, create a simple poster/chart for read alouds. One possible example might look like figure 5.5, but remember, your chart should be based on the needs of your children. Let the children help in the creation and make it easily accessible for your nonreaders. Refer to the chart before read alouds, reducing the number of times you reference it in a week as the children become more versed in the routine of read alouds.

You will want to revisit the chart if children need reminders or if they want to add something to make the read aloud experience more enjoyable. Just remember, this is a chart that changes as the needs of the children change and as you learn together about what makes an enjoyable read aloud.

Figure 5.5   Child-created guide for read alouds

Consider the Crowd

You can read aloud to the whole class and to small crowds of children. When reading aloud to the whole class, it is still important to gather the children as close to you as possible. This is the most prevalent way that read alouds are conducted in classrooms. Because the crowds may be large and proximity to the book and teacher may not be ideal, it is easy for children to disengage from the read aloud. Be especially aware of each child to ensure that everyone can:

- See the illustrations
- Hear the words
- Watch the reader's movements and reactions
- Ask and respond to questions
- Make predictions and connections

In figure 5.6, Ghida Hijazi is modeling what this might look like. Can you see the note on the book reminding her of questions she wants to ask children?

Figure 5.6 Ghida Hijazi reading aloud in her classroom

While you might spend the majority of your time in whole class read alouds, you should spend time reading to small crowds as well. When reading aloud in small crowds, ideally not more than six, conversations are often deeper and more individualized. Small crowd read alouds may be done simply because a group of children shares an interest in a book title and all want to hear it at the same time. In addition, you may invite children to a small crowd read aloud experience in order to meet the critical literacy needs of those specific children.

An often-neglected format for reading aloud in classrooms is reading *alongside* an individual child. "In this individualized time between the adult and child, it is possible to follow the child's questions and understandings about the story and about how text works. One to one conversations such as these inform a teacher's perspective on a child's reading development" (Short, 2011, p. 58).

For an *alongside* read aloud experience, young children can select a text of individual interest. This provides you with an opportunity to focus more on reading comprehension in an authentic way (Sanacore, 2002). It may also be the perfect place for you to engage those children who may not be as interested in the whole crowd read aloud. We know from Ledger and Merga (2018) that a small minority of children may not like whole crowd read alouds because they:

- Want to read on their own
- Do not like the book selections
- Are turned off by teachers who read with little inflection, or
- Are bothered by the talk that happens during the reading

The *alongside* read aloud allows you to take cues from the child about when to share the reading and to talk about meaning. Consider how you might use *alongside* read alouds to promote conversation, questioning, connection, and so on and think about how your ideas fit with the example read aloud (figure 5.7).

One final note to consider is that if the majority of the children are inattentive or seem bored with a read aloud, you may want to evaluate your reading style. If you are not engaging listeners with

- character voices,
- whispering during sad or scary parts,
- louder voices on exciting parts,
- adjustments of speed for slow or fast moments, and
- modeling and soliciting good questioning, connecting, and interesting responses,

then the problem may be the reader and not the listeners. Pay close attention to how you read and how engaged the children are during the read aloud. Adjust what you are doing based upon reactions from the listeners.

Discuss the Read Aloud

Once you have prepared for the read aloud environment and organization, it is important to spend some time thinking about two often-overlooked components of read alouds: inquiry and discussion. "An inquiry stance to literature and curriculum invites children to make meaning of texts in personally and culturally significant ways to facilitate learning and to develop lifelong reading attitudes and habit" (Short, 2011, p. 60).

Children are naturally curious, which leads to inquiry. The best way to encourage inquiry is through discussion. Sometimes you can plan for discussions, but other times children may select a book for an impromptu read aloud. Whether you have time to plan for the read aloud or not, you have to be actively listening to and observing the children in order to encourage talk and inquiry.

If possible, plan at least one open-ended question for your read aloud and then let the children lead the conversation. The key to remember is that you are steering the dialogue and co-constructing meaning with the children. Listen carefully and keep the discussion going by asking follow-up questions that encourage connections to schema and the text evidence, like:

- Why do you feel that way?
- Why do you think that happened?
- What would you have done?
- Why do you think the author chose to write that?

It is not enough to just ask open-ended questions. It is about scaffolding so that children are using their schema and the text to enhance the discussion and validate meaning. The more we read, talk, and inquire, the better developed our background knowledge (schema).

Sometimes "difficult" conversations might emerge through the read aloud dialogue. Don't be afraid of these, even with young children. Books that promote inquiry about issues like loss, injustice, and death should not be avoided because of fear about what children might feel. These types of texts provide a safe space to learn about life. And, because you are a trusted caregiver, children will find comfort as they learn about these important life lessons.

Research tells us that young children can navigate these types of texts and conversations. While Hohr's (2000) research specifically investigated the impact of fairy tales, it astutely illustrates how a story "lures the child onto the playground of hurtful and fearful emotions, enables him or her to play through them symbolically, and promises to lead him or her onto stable ground again, unhurt and relieved" (p. 100).

BOX 5.3 OBSERVE A READ ALOUD IN ACTION

Text: *City Dog, Country Frog* by Mo Willems & Jon J. Muth

Step 1: Begin by reading the title and the author/illustrator. This is always important because you want children to know titles so that they can request them for rereads, and you want them to know the author and illustrator so that they can request other books created by them.

Step 2: Move to talking to the children about the cover of the book, asking them to predict what they think the book is about. Make sure to allow enough wait time between questions that you ask.

> Example: "What do you see in the picture? Do you see City Dog and Country Frog? Why do you think Country Frog is sitting on City Dog's head?"

Step 3: Picture walk the book (looking at the illustrations but not reading the text) before reading to offer opportunities for prediction. You might walk to the front matter page (before the story begins) that shows four images from the book and ask what students notice about those images. Talk about the fact that each represents a season, and prepare the readers for the idea that the story is told based on moments in Spring, Summer, Fall, and Winter. Remember, conversation before reading aloud is essential, but do not feel compelled to talk about every page. Use your own judgment to find the pages that activate schema for essential parts of the story.

Step 4: Read the book and model. Throughout, ponder questions and offer possible answers, using schema and the text to support those possibilities. Make your own connections and inferences as well. All of this serves as a model for what readers do. You have to find that perfect balance between the right amount of modeling and too much interruption. Again, use your judgment about the modeling that best meets the needs of children.

> Example: "I wonder why City Dog was so excited to be able to run without a leash. Oh, he is a city dog. He probably has to walk on a leash every day. He doesn't have big fields to run in where he lives."

Step 5: Keep reading, stopping to pose purposeful questions to promote connections that will allow the children to make inferences about parts of the story. As children relate to what is read, they think about experiences that they have had and liken them to what is happening to characters in the book. On one page, City Dog tells Country Frog that they will play City Dog games.

> Example: "What types of games do you think a city dog would play? What kinds of games did Country Frog play first? Why are they different?"

Questions like these should be thoughtful and allow the reader to contemplate the text more deeply. They should promote dialogue with the children. It's about co-constructing meaning. But . . . it is about enjoyment too.

Step 6: While reading aloud, pay close attention to your prosody, which includes elements like tone and inflection. The way that you project your voice and body adds life to the read aloud. For instance, in the story, the second time City Dog visits Country Frog, he runs straight to the rock without stopping. This scene prompts you to read the text a bit more quickly with excitement. At the end of the book, when City Dog cannot find Country Frog, you may want to slow down and project worry or concern about the dilemma.

Step 7: Don't neglect the important dialogue that will take place at the end of the book. The ending is left open to interpretation, and most children will experience the emotions that Willems and Muth so covertly infuse into the writing and illustrations. These emotional undertones, along with the concept of friendship introduced in the book, encourage discussions that prompt empathy. When Country Frog does not return to the pond, discussion leads the children to connect to experiences where a friendship has changed; e.g., a friend has moved, a family member has not returned, or other feelings of loss.

> Example: Most children will ask, "Where is Country Frog?" You can prompt them to discuss where he might be, like he found another friend to play with, he moved to another pond, and so on. Ask the children to justify their evidence with their own schema about these possibilities. If a child asks if Country Frog died, you can follow up with "What makes you think that?" Leave the debate to the children; walk them back through the text evidence to enhance their discussion.

Inevitably, many children will determine that Country Frog died. If a child says, "My maw maw died," you can respond, "Oh, I'm so sorry to hear that. My grandmother died when I was young too."

These are the hard, but important, conversations that we mentioned earlier. This type of discussion, although difficult at first, allows the child to feel comfortable enough to open up to you. It also proves that

> stories evoke strong emotions within us that can help us better relate to problems of our time. It also makes a strong connection to the world around by showing that we are not alone; difficult things happen to all. Great stories are sometimes just the thing we need to help us through difficult situations.

No matter whether you choose to read aloud to a whole crowd, small crowd, or *alongside* a child, it is about the enjoyment and the discussion, sharing the experience together. Prioritize daily, delightful read alouds as an imperative part of teaching literacy. Children must have a love for reading that evokes memories of fondness and understand that reading is about making meaning, and you, as the teacher, are just the person who can provide the space for that engaging, joyful, and warm experience.

Principle 6

Use Children's Texts to Teach Content

When you walk into an early childhood classroom, you expect to see children learning important content through iZones (introduced in principle 4) filled with lots of books. Simply filling the iZone with books, however, does not guarantee content learning. So, how do educators expertly teach content through children's texts (fiction, nonfiction, periodical, or reference texts)?

Imagine that children have an interest in flowers, and they build iZones around that theme. What types of books and materials might be included, and how are children using them?

The books might include *Sunflower House* by Eve Bunting, *van Gogh and the Sunflowers* by Laurence Anholt, and *A Sunflower's Life Cycle* by Mary R. Dunn. There are diagrams and models of sunflowers, copies of van Gogh's art, painter's smocks, paints, paper, and more. On the computer, children are investigating sunflowers on websites like Britannica Kids and Science News for Students. The children are noticing the sizes and shapes of sunflowers, the colors of the flowers, and even the intricate details about seed pods. They are intentionally using books as models to inform the flower art that they are about to create.

Too many times, we are satisfied to pull texts that are related to a theme, yet we never truly show the children how to purposefully use those texts. The children in the example had a reason to use the texts because they were preparing to paint flower art. Most importantly, and something not as evident, is that they knew how to use the texts to get the information needed to create that art.

TALK ABOUT USING CHILDREN'S TEXTS IN IZONES

Meet Brittany and Vonthisha, two first-grade teachers, who are considering texts for a new iZone (figure 6.1). Pay close attention to why they select the books that they do.

Notice how Brittany and Vonthisha made it a point to indicate titles that could promote specific activities to enhance content learning. Not only will the children learn about science content in this iZone, but the two teachers are integrating opportunities for authentic literacy learning. After selecting texts that promote content learning, the next step for Brittany and Vonthisha will be to teach the children how to purposefully use those texts.

iZones provide perfect spaces for giving your children opportunity to demonstrate content learning through authentic, purposeful activities. But, the

Brittany: The children have been so excited about pond habitats since our trip to the Arboretum Nature Center last week.

Vonthisha: Mine are the same. We started an anchor chart today of what they are interested in learning and what materials they want to use. Tomorrow, I will bring in items for the iZone that they can use to build and explore pond habitats both in the classroom and in the outdoor play area.

Brittany: Ok, I will start a chart with my children as well. Maybe we can have our classes work together to build the pond play area outdoors.

Vonthisha: Yes, that's a great idea. Do you have any thoughts about which texts might fit into this iZone?

Brittany: We definitely need nonfiction texts and periodicals so that they can learn more about ponds and the animals and plants that live there. *Life in the Pond* by Craig Hammersmith might be a good book to help the children start a pond encyclopedia.

Vonthisha: How about *In the Small, Small Pond* by Denise Fleming? This is fiction and uses alliteration as it shows the reader animals that might be living around a pond. The children could use it as a mentor text and add alliteration to field guides they create for our pond.

Brittany: *Turtle Splash! Countdown at the Pond* by Cathryn Falwell would also be great. The children can critically analyze the animals mentioned in this counting book to determine if they really would be in a pond habitat.

Vonthisha: That's a great start. I will ask the librarian both here and at the public library for additional titles that the children can purposefully use in the iZone.

Figure 6.1 A little talk about using children's texts in iZones

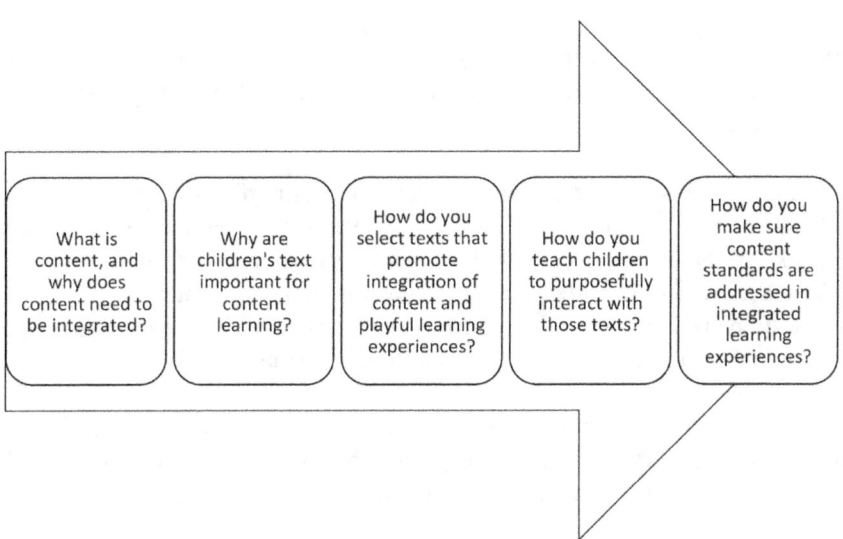

Figure 6.2 Questions to frame your understanding of principle 6

focus of this principle will not be on activities. Instead, you will learn more about the term "content" and discover why integration of content is necessary. You will explore the importance of purposefully selecting and using children's texts in iZones and be introduced to methods and strategies that allow children to intentionally use those texts to learn content. Figure 6.2 provides questions that will guide your thinking as you read. Consider keeping track of the answers as you discover them.

CONSIDER CONTENT LEARNING

What is content? Content areas are the different subjects that we teach, like math, science, reading, writing, and social studies. In many classrooms, content is taught as segregated topics, but it doesn't have to be that way. Literacy, specifically, is very easy to pair with other content areas.

Why does content need to be integrated? Everyday life is integrated; it's as simple as that. "To prepare students for career readiness, we must emphasize that authentic problems and experiences are multifaceted and not constricted to 45-minute blocks" (Larson & Rumsey, 2017, p. 589). We encourage you to be innovative when thinking about content integration. So, instead of viewing language arts as its own block, math as another block taught later, and science and social studies as the block that comes at the end of the day, think about how to teach the content together.

An iZone provides the perfect place for children to explore content in integrated, natural ways through the use of children's play and texts. Neuman (2014) offers principles for you to consider when teaching integrated content through iZones:

- Large amounts of content can be linked to meaningful concepts.
- Concept links assist learners in making necessary schematic connections.
- Links are taught through both direct and exploratory instruction.
- Teachers scaffold children through questioning and discourse.
- Children are gradually released to more complex thinking and are provided essential opportunities to engage and link concepts.

Figure 6.3 spotlights two first-grade teachers who use integration daily in their classroom. Notice how Brandy and Courtney are purposeful about the inclusion of texts in varied learning situations.

PURPOSEFULLY SELECT *JUST RIGHT* TEXTS FOR CONTENT LEARNING IN IZONES

Why are children's texts important for content learning? They serve as scaffolds for merging new information into schema. Children's texts also:

- Allow children to study content from different perspectives
- Offer more time to be immersed in content areas that often get neglected
- Improve engagement and motivation
- Make learning content fun (Hindin, 2018; Larson & Rumsey, 2017).

How do you select texts that promote integration of content and playful learning experiences? The texts you select should engage children and inspire them to want to know more about a topic. They are texts that get a lot of attention and appeal to your children. These texts must be:

- Balanced by genre
- Oriented toward critical evaluation of content
- Aligned with interests

Balance Fiction with Nonfiction

In your iZones, fictional texts offer children opportunities to live vicariously in a world where they can pretend to be someone else or see themselves in the

Spotlight on Practice

Brandy Green and Courtney Fuhrken

First-Grade Teachers

Using books to teach literacy skills
Brandy: Part of our job is to get kids to believe they are readers and writers. When you immerse them in literature, they make connections. Kids naturally point out skills like phonemic awareness and phonics.

Courtney: Literacy is a springboard to teach almost anything. Even when teaching phonemic awareness or phonics, you can still refer to literature. We want them to read like a writer and write like a reader. So, we try to put literature in everything. In poetry, in guided reading, in every part of the reading workshop. We make connections with other texts. We tell the kids, "This is like the story we read." We are changing the way they think about books, but we have to be purposeful.

Purposefully choosing books for learning stations
Courtney: I put books in stations that have plenty of rhymes for the kids. They have a buddy reading station, a library station, a listening station, and an independent reading station where they can choose what to read. They have leveled readers but also books by interest. The children are reading and listening to books being read. They are also having discussions about the books in those stations.

Brandy: We are really focusing on oral language, and we want them to talk. For science and social studies concepts, we take pictures and put them in the oral language station. That way the children can continue academic talk. For example, we did this when we studied lakes, oceans, deserts, and forests. When we listen to kids in stations, they are having some really good conversations. Sometimes readers respond to books in their reader's notebook. There is also a word study station with books so they are looking for patterns in words they are studying. They are still reading as they are searching. They have a poem station with poems that we have read. They love them!

Using books to teach other content
Courtney: We try to pair books with science concepts or use nonfiction for shared reading. We do the same thing for math. We have to integrate as much as possible and be intentional. The intentional piece changes the way you teach. We see students dabbling in integration throughout the day. It sparks their imagination. They wonder, imagine, and talk about content. They go home and do research with their parents and then come back and report to us. I've seen our children want to read more and more nonfiction. They want to read and write about what they learn.

Brandy: We pair shared reading and poems with content like science. For example, if we are studying the life cycle of a frog, our poem might be about the life cycle of a frog or shared reading would be about the frog with a nonfiction book. In math, we choose books that are related to what we are teaching like a counting book. Integration sets such a good foundation, widens their viewpoint, and opens them up to a whole new world.

Figure 6.3 Spotlight on practice: Courtney Fuhrken and Brandy Green, first-grade teachers

lives of others. Fiction also can scaffold for the heaviness of content concepts, which will make tackling nonfiction much easier.

Perhaps *The Storm Whale* by Benji Davies is already in your library collection, and your children have selected it for their iZone about ocean animals. This fictional story could introduce the children to vocabulary like *sea*, *ocean*, and *beach*. In addition, important concepts like a whale needing to be in the water and eating fish might be of interest to readers.

Maybe the book *The Blue Whale* by Jenni Desmond is also included as an informational book in this iZone. When children read about the blue whale, they will learn about feeding habits like its diet of krill. The children might question why the whale in *The Storm Whale* ate fish and why the blue whale eats krill, which will lead to further exploration and analysis about the eating habits of all types of whales.

The readers might also learn that, at birth, a blue whale calf is about twenty-five feet long. This may cause readers to question how the Storm Whale could fit in a bathtub, leading to study of varying weights and lengths of different whale species. The idea is that the nonfiction text provided new, accurate information about whales while at the same time challenging some ideas presented in the fictional story. The fiction and nonfiction texts worked together to enhance schematic knowledge about whales.

Just like the ocean animals theme can benefit from both fiction and nonfiction texts, so too can a theme like fairy tales. For example, if children read Will Moses's version of *Hansel and Gretel*, it might prompt questions like:

- What is a woodcutter?
- How big is a cottage, and where do people live in cottages?
- Can you really make a house from candy? Would I be able to live in it?
- Would a duck be big enough for me to ride?
- Are there other versions of Hansel and Gretel's story?

These important questions can best be answered with nonfiction texts, periodicals, or reference books. Having only fiction in a fairy tale iZone would deny children the opportunity to explore other content and learn from other genres.

Evaluate the Content in Children's Texts

When you select texts for content in iZones, carefully consider authenticity. Too often in children's texts, we see inaccurate or misleading representations of content concepts. Both you and your children need to become expert fact checkers. Here are some key issues that savvy readers should avoid:

⚠ Avoid thinking that all authors are experts in the content. Read the author biography to determine whether or not that author has authority on the content

⚠ Avoid assuming that just because it's in writing, it is true. Be curious about the details of books and use resources inside and outside of the text to confirm or reject facts

⚠ Avoid overlooking extreme language. Understand terms like always, never, and everyone and analyze whether or not that extreme exaggeration holds any truth

A famous example can be found in *The Very Hungry Caterpillar* by Eric Carle. In this fictional story, the caterpillar goes into a *cocoon* to transform into a butterfly. The reality is that butterflies emerge from a chrysalis; moths emerge from a cocoon.

Nonfiction books can fall victim to misinformation too. Gill (n.d.) discusses issues with accuracy in nonfiction texts. Her article is a great resource for comprehensive tips for analyzing the accuracy of children's books.

Another resource that can help you learn how to evaluate content in nonfiction texts is from Kylene Beers and Robert Probst. *Reading Nonfiction: Notice and Notes, Stances, Signposts, and Strategies* (2016) is a professional development book dedicated to different methods for questioning nonfiction. This book helps you consider your own ability to evaluate content in texts and apply it to how you teach even the youngest readers to evaluate facts.

Include Taxonomic Texts

Some research has shown that content knowledge, along with vocabulary acquisition, can be enhanced by using taxonomic texts, stories that represent information in a natural context, for example, birds sleeping in nests instead of a bed as humans would. These taxonomic texts give children a chance to make comparisons with existing knowledge. They help scaffold children's thinking and often assist with real-world connections.

In a study that investigated read alouds where the reader did not engage in dialogue with children and the text served as the only scaffold, Pinkham, Kaefer, and Neuman (2014) found that "children may have been able to acquire new vocabulary from the taxonomic storybook, but not the traditional storybook, without receiving extratextual scaffolding from an adult reader" (p. 5). For non-taxonomic texts, it seems that the book alone cannot provide the complete scaffold for the children; you are still an important part of that process. The ideal scaffold would be taxonomic stories combined with teacher questioning and guidance.

We have to ensure that we clarify any dissonance that the children might experience when a text is not taxonomic. For example, you can definitely read Froggy books by Jonathan London; they are humorous stories about a young frog who has very similar experiences to children, like learning to swim, first sleepovers, and a first kiss.

Because Froggy lives in a house, sleeps in a bed, and wears clothing, we have to take care about including these books in a content study about amphibians. Having children compare and discuss what they are learning about real frogs, frog habitats, and so on with Froggy is a good way to ease any schematic dissonance that they may feel.

Align the Texts with Interest

"Whether teachers are selecting texts for whole-class readings or planning experiences to expand content knowledge, it is important that they consider children's interests" (Hindin, 2018, p. 173). Look for diverse texts that present the iZone's theme in a fascinating way. Consider letting the children guide you in the kinds of texts you choose. Ask yourself:

- How do the topic, words, and illustrations stimulate, capture, and hold children's attention?
- What do the words offer the children in terms of rich vocabulary that relate to content?
- How is the content connected, and/or does the text integrate several content areas? For example: science, language, art, and math.
- What are the opportunities for children to make connections, ask questions, and infer?
- How does the text push them forward in their interest and learning about the topic?

Many teachers will survey children to find out about interests. You can create your own interest survey, based on the level of your children. You might consider interviews or picture surveys if your children are very young. After you gather the data that you need, you will want to align interest with the iZone theme. Here are a few resources that might help you with that alignment:

- Reading Rockets has lists of books that fit with identified themes
- Scholastic has Ready-to-Go Book Lists for Teachers organized by grade and theme
- Scholastic also offers a list of Great Picture Books to Teach Social Studies

- Math Reads by Marilyn Burns aligns books to math standards through a comprehensive program
- National Science Teaching Association (NSTA) provides lists of outstanding books. They are not organized into themes, but the list gives a good sampling of rich content connections
- National Council of Teachers of English (NCTE) awards nonfiction texts each year (Orbus Pictus) and houses extensive lists of past winners and honor books

Although searching for optimal texts to promote content is not always an easy task, the benefits for the children are too numerous to ignore. We must find texts that promote content in the most relevant ways to guarantee that a multitude of rich resources make their way into the iZones.

PURPOSEFULLY SUPPORT YOUNG READERS AS THEY INTERACT WITH TEXTS IN IZONES

Finding *just right* texts for content learning is not enough, however. Children have to learn how to *use* texts to enhance content understanding. Too often, we see learning centers filled with books that are not *really* being used (Catapano, Fleming, & Elias, 2009). This is unfortunate, books lining the shelves of classroom libraries just waiting to be given purpose.

How do you teach children to purposefully interact with those texts? One way teachers can promote focused inquiry about content topics is by teaching children to read and reread closely.

Teach Close Reading through a Process

Close reading involves digging deeply into the meaning of a complex text and often requires rereading. It is a pretty sophisticated way to interact with texts, so you will want to do much modeling and supporting of your young readers so that they build reading strength for these types of texts.

While initially a strategy addressed at the secondary level, primary teachers can and do effectively teach close reading to children (Fisher & Frey, 2012; 2014). Close reading can "integrate these habits within the context of a more difficult piece of text" and help children to understand (Fisher & Frey, 2012, p. 180):

- Text organization
- Vocabulary

- Argument
- Key details
- Inferential meaning
- Author's purpose
- Text to text connections
- Synthesis of information from the text with schema to form new ideas

Figure 6.4 introduces a process we are calling *READ* (Read, Engage, Ask, and Document) when teaching close reading:

- *R*ead the text for pleasure and then model rereading closely.
  - This could be done with whole groups as shared reading and with smaller groups of children in the iZones, but you can also do this in *alongside* reading. Be sure to think aloud and annotate with drawings or simple words to show discoveries that you make.
  - Think about the gradual release model (Pearson & Gallagher, 1983). You will have all or most of the responsibility for reading the text in this first part of the process.
- *E*ngage individual children in close reading practice by scaffolding in the iZone.

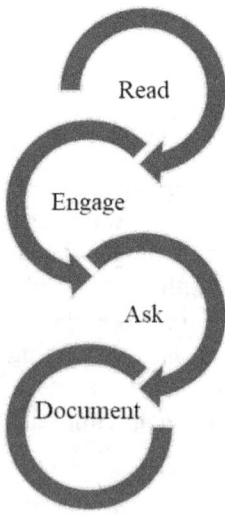

Figure 6.4 A process to follow when teaching close reading

- This provides an opportunity to individualize close reading instruction. Be aware of how much scaffolding you do initially because you want the reader to do most of the thinking. Use text-dependent questions to encourage the reader to dig into the text for answers. Encourage the reader to use illustrations or simple words to note discoveries made.
- This is the place in the gradual release model where you are giving over most, but not quite all, of the reading responsibility to children.
- *A*sk children to reinvestigate the text without teacher scaffolding to promote deeper practice with close reading.
  - This is the moment in the process where you release the responsibility for reading to the children.
- *D*ocument when children effectively use close reading.
  - This should be evident when children purposefully use an iZone text to display content learning; if children are having trouble reading closely, begin the process again.

As you can see, the *READ* process naturally fosters that relationship between the teacher and the children where the children lead the teacher through the text. The teacher facilitates the learning through scaffolding and supports the children's thinking.

Consider an Example of How to READ Closely

Let's think about using *READ* with *Tuesday* by David Wiesner. *Tuesday* is a very detailed, visual wordless picture book. The illustrations tell the story and seem to come to life on the page. Since the book has so much pictorial detail, it lends itself to close rereading and great discussion.

Read the text first for enjoyment, engaging the children in dialogue about the text, just as you learned in principle 5. Then, model close reading.

For your model, find one thing in the book that would require close analysis. You might reread the end and notice that there are pigs flying. You ask and document on a sticky note, "Why didn't the pigs fly with the frogs?" Then, you reread the first few pages and notice that the frogs were flying, but the turtle wasn't; use another sticky note to document this. A closer reading of these pages reveals that the frogs are flying *this* Tuesday, while the pigs are flying *next* Tuesday. Use highlighter tape to note the words *this* and *next*. That leads to a determination that different animals fly on different Tuesdays.

Engage in scaffolded assistance in the iZone. The children study a particular part of the text that interests them and talk about what is happening in the illustrations. Remember, let the children do most of the thinking. For example, the children might notice that the clouds are in the shape of frogs on lily pads. You might ask, "Why do you think the clouds look like frogs? Is there something in the text to help you?"

Guide the children to really investigate the images of the frogs flying in the text; they might want to draw what they see. Then, encourage them to study the images of the frogs when they are not flying, again drawing what they see. Ask, "How do you think they feel in those pictures?" The children should notice that the frogs are happy when flying and sad when not flying. Perhaps the clouds are representative of the way that the frogs feel when they fly, like they are on cloud nine. Your job is to guide them to their conclusions.

After sufficient scaffolding, *ask* the children to try close reading on their own. Observe them, but let them do the reading and thinking. For example, on his own, a child may reread to notice that the sun is coming up on the page where the frogs are falling off the lily pads. He might say, "Look, it must be the next morning. Tuesday was the evening; it's Wednesday in that picture, so they don't get to fly." The child is mastering the close reading approach.

Determine the best way to record and document this mastery. Be sure to notice children who have not mastered the approach, and go back through the *READ* process of modeling, scaffolding, and allowing for independent practice.

TEACH SPECIFIC STRATEGIES CHILDREN CAN USE DURING CLOSE READING

Let's think about the specific strategies that children need in order to read closely, like in the *Tuesday* example. These strategies empower children as they assimilate new information from purposeful texts.

Scaffold Background Knowledge

Young readers need to access the background knowledge necessary for content learning. Sometimes they need you to help them *make connections* to what they already know about the content. For example, if you read aloud *Trombone Shorty* by Troy "Trombone Shorty" Andrews and plan to add this book to a jazz music iZone, some children might benefit from looking back at the instruments they have already investigated and discussing how the trombone is the same as or different from what they already know.

Fill in Gaps

Sometimes children need you to *fill in gaps* in their schematic knowledge. Because the setting of Trombone Shorty is New Orleans, it might be important for some children to reference a map and talk about the culture of this city, especially related to jazz. Show images from the city. Play a song, like "Hurricane Season" by Andrews, and talk about the music.

There is great "variability in children's preexisting knowledge [that] may profoundly impact their subsequent learning" (Pinkham, Kaefer, & Neuman, 2014, p. 7). In this case, introducing them to the sounds of jazz music and the sights of the city of New Orleans will scaffold them for *Trombone Shorty* and might prompt the children to search for similar information about other musicians that they will study in the iZone later.

If you find you are lacking knowledge about a particular topic, you will need to research and stock your own schematic deficits. Look for information in various forms of texts. Don't underestimate periodicals. They can offer detailed information on particular topics and can be easy to read. For example, "U.S. History: Jazz" on Ducksters Education site might fill your schema and also be read aloud and placed in the iZone for your children.

Ask Questions

Another strategy that enables children to read closely is questioning. Teach children to use questions to *discover something completely new* and *research words and ideas*.

Discover Something Completely New

In *Trombone Shorty*, Andrews plays his trombone with Bo Diddley at a very young age. Young readers may not know the significance of this moment because they lack schema for Bo Diddley. You might ask aloud, "Who is Bo Diddley? Why does Trombone Shorty think that moment was so important?"

These questions encourage children to research Bo Diddley and the very moment that Trombone Shorty played with him. Your model helps children to learn that simply reading the text and skipping over information that is not understood is not what readers do. Instead, the strategy highlights the importance of being a curious reader.

Research Words and Ideas

In addition, teach students to be careful consumers of books and *question like researchers*. Some nonfiction authors unintentionally use obscure language, even in expository texts. For example, in *Animals Nobody Loves*, Seymour Simon states, "The most dangerous shark is the great white shark" (p. 8). There are, in reality, three sharks (the great white, tiger, and bull shark) that are repeatedly implicated in shark attacks (Florida Museum of Natural History's International Shark Attack File, 2019). The great white, however, does have the most fatalities for unprovoked attacks.

So, what does *dangerous*, as Simon indicated, mean? If it means fatalities, then Simon's statement might be factual. If it means attacks, then two other sharks should likely be considered in the most dangerous list. The point is that it is very complicated to determine which shark is the most *dangerous*. Young readers might not always be able to point out this type of language used in nonfiction texts, but teaching them how to do it at a young age will get them on their way to being readers who are researchers.

Also, many children's nonfiction books are written with a narrative style. Often, authors take some liberties with that style and blur the lines between facts that can be verified and those that cannot. *Ivan: The Remarkable True Story of the Shopping Mall Gorilla* has examples of the liberties that Applegate takes with this nonfiction text. The first page reads, "In leafy calm, in gentle arms, a gorilla's life began." The "leafy calm" and "gentle arms" represent beautiful language that starts the reader on the journey of Ivan's story. However, we cannot verify that this is how Ivan experienced the beginnings of life.

Narrative nonfiction is important for young readers because it helps them live in the world of some really complex topics. We do not want to discount its value in the early childhood classroom, but we do want teachers to address these issues with young readers so that they grow in their ability to distinguish between literary license and facts when they are engaging in close reading.

Teach the Features of Nonfiction Texts

A third strategy that children need for close reading is the ability to use text features to gather information. Often expository texts are designed with intriguing illustrations, unique captions, colorful charts, graphs, or other images that must be read. These fact-based texts shed a whole new light on learning content through close reading. Teach children to follow these steps:

1. Skim the book to look for unique text features that provide support or additional information.
2. Read the additional text provided that is located in the unique features; note (paper clips, sticky notes, drawings, etc.) interesting information not seen when reading the main text of the book.
3. Reread the pages that are marked, compare them to the main text, and record with words or pictures the new information learned.

Consider the expository text *Pink Is for Blobfish* by Jess Keating. This book contains lots of organized pictures and graphic information along with main text to help children learn more about pink animals. Children will likely first read the main text and skip the text found in side bars, graphics, captions, and so on. On the pages about the Blobfish, reading the main text just gives basic information. Closely rereading the additional text gives more details (like species, size, habitat) and some unique, humorous information (like the Blobfish was nominated ugliest animal).

Notice and Access Unknown Words

New words can be intimidating. Vocabulary doesn't just jump off the page and become embedded in our minds. It has to be nurtured, developed, and grown. We have the power to encourage children to cultivate their knowledge of vocabulary during close reading by providing texts that are rich with words and promoting discussion of those words. Teach children how to identify words they may not know as they read.

- Don't overlook unfamiliar words. Just like children should not overlook questions that they have, they also cannot overlook unfamiliar words.
- Use context to determine meaning. Search pictures and other words unknown to help uncover meaning.
- Compare new words to known words or word parts. For example, if a child knows the meaning of *unkind*, he might apply knowledge of "un" to *unattached* to determine that the new word means not attached.
- Talk about and discuss the meaning of the word with others. When children work together, they support each other in word meaning analysis.
- Document new words in a notebook or on a notepad to research in other texts.

Once children feel comfortable with the strategy of identifying difficult vocabulary, they will automatically use context clues, word analysis, research, and talk for words they find difficult during close reading.

LINK READING TEXTS AND LEARNING CONTENT WITH STANDARDS

How do you make sure content standards are addressed in integrated learning experiences? Aligning texts, reading experiences, content learning, and standards can seem like an enormous task at first when you consider all of the skills children must master in one year. In addition, thinking about how to align all of this within a theme that permeates iZone play might feel daunting. But, breathe. The key is small steps.

- Know your state and school standards. Note the degree to which your children should master the skills.
- Identify DAP.
- Discern the interests and needs of your children.
- Develop play-based themes for learning content.
- Check your classroom library for titles that address the content and interests of your children.
- Read the texts selected.
- Identify content skills that can be addressed with the text.
- Determine how to teach children to use those texts purposefully as they learn the content.
- Develop authentic activities to expand text and content understanding.

You might consider creating a chart similar to table 6.1. Start by evaluating one book at a time. Before you know it, you will have developed your own individualized, thematically based content plans that allow you to differentiate for the needs and interests of the children in your classroom.

As you can see in table 6.1 planning the alignment of content to skills and standards can take some time. Practice will help you to envision ideas to accompany books, see the skills and standards embedded in those ideas, and, then, grow those ideas into detailed activities that encourage children to learn new information and apply it to their own thinking. We urge you to practice with the additional book ideas in table 6.1.

Look back at figure 6.2. Did you discover the answers to the questions in the notes that you took? Our hope is that this principle showed you how to individualize your thematic iZones through developmentally appropriate ideas that align texts, content, and standards. Most importantly, we hope that you learned how to select purposeful texts with the children in mind, letting children guide your choices.

Table 6.1 Examples of how to align content-rich texts, themes, and standards

iZone Theme	Inventors
First Book to Analyze	*Balloons over Broadway: The True Story of the Puppeteer of Macy's Parade* by Melissa Sweet
Examples of Integrated, Skills-Based Ideas to Accompany the Book	What skills-based ideas could children engage in because this book is in the iZone? 1. Literacy (Comprehension/Getting Ready for Further Content Learning and Exploration): Close reading strategies of nonfiction text structure and features (reading/rereading narrative nonfiction, illustrations, captions, labels, bylines, and extra text: author's notes and periodicals); using vocabulary strategies to give meaning to unknown words (marionette, puppeteers, helium, blimp, shimmied, flounced, gestured, articulated); filling schematic deficits through images and discussion (Macy's and their parade, New York City, Herald Square, Macy's window puppets, parade balloons, Central Park Zoo) 2. Geography, history, literacy, math (Digging Deeper into Time and Place): Reading about and discussing places (London, New York City, and Ohio) and locating these on a map; measuring the distance between New York City and Ohio using the scale on the map; using a map to locate the parade route from 110th to 34th streets in New York City and comparing the distance to a familiar route children know; read about, discuss, watch videos about, and listen to music from 1928 and compare this to the current year; read about the origin of Thanksgiving; use an analog clock to tell time and discuss the times mentioned in the book by listing activities that children do during those times 3. Literacy, art (Digging Deeper into Art): Discussing what Sweet meant by playing with art; practicing playing with art (different textures, materials, styles); analyzing Sweet's collages; and creating their own collages 4. Science, art, literacy, drama, math (The Puppet Show): Reading about, viewing videos, and discussing the way things move (pulleys, levers, fulcrum); experimenting with physics (e.g., how to create an invention to open a door from far away, like is done in the book); experimenting with creation of self-portrait puppet; creating illustrated/written plans for experiment, puppet designs, and puppet show; measuring materials for invention and puppets; illustrating/writing scripts for puppet show where their puppet tells about an event from his life

Continued

Table 6.1 (Continued)

Standards Related to Skills-Based Ideas	What standards are addressed through the skills-based ideas? Note, these are compiled from both the Common Core State Standards (http://www.corestandards.org/read-the-standards/) and Texas Essential Knowledge and Skills (https://tea.texas.gov/curriculum/teks/) for Grade 2:
	1. Literacy: Question, understand key details; connect concepts and events; determine word meaning by choosing from strategies; know and use various text features and images to locate and clarify key facts or information (CCSS); follow rules to listening and speaking and build on those experiences; write with topics/facts to inform or explain; write with narrative sequence, detail, and craft; participate in shared research where information must be gathered; tell a story with visuals, appropriate sentence complexity, and audible speech
	2. Math: Measure length, compare lengths, generate measurement data, apply math problems to everyday life, show and talk about mathematical ideas using content vocabulary, tell and write time
	3. Science: Identify a problem and pose a solution, plan and conduct investigation, record data, communicate results, combine materials together to create something new that could not be created with the individual materials
	4. Social Studies: Understand holidays and traditions, identify tools that help determine location, describe customs and traditions and determine similarities and differences among those, obtain information about topics, create and interpret visuals
	5. Drama: React to experiences through dramatic play, plan and create limited dramatizations, imitate life experiences through dramatic play
	6. Art: Identify elements of art, express personal feelings in artwork
Conduct a Text & Standard Alignment Plan with These Additional Book Ideas	What other texts might I include in the iZone to address the topic of inventors? • *The Hole Story of the Doughnut* by Pat Miller • *Mr. Ferris and His Wheel* by Kathryn Gibbs Davis • *Joseph Had a Little Overcoat* by Simms Taback • *The Three Little Pigs* by James Marshall • *The Most Magnificent Thing* by Ashely Spires

The ultimate goal for text use in iZones is for students to be able to read and understand so that they are able to apply that knowledge to purposeful content activities. That application leads to deeper, more authentic content learning.

Principle 7

Cultivate Literacy Skills with Balanced Instruction

Teaching literacy to even the youngest children requires both explicit and implicit instruction. Explicit instruction implies that information is presented without confusion. It is "direct. . . [and] proceeds in small steps, supporting learning through instructional supports and scaffolds and fostering active participation and response" (Reutzel & Cooter, 2019, pp. 180–190). When you teach children explicitly, think about:

- Focusing on smaller parts of critical skills or strategies (teaching easier parts before harder parts; making sure children have schema for those parts before you teach)
- Modeling how to interact with those smaller parts (stating specifically the skill or strategy and the objective for learning)
- Releasing the scaffolded support gradually (knowing how quickly to release that support)
- Answering questions and clarifying confusions specifically related to the smaller parts (giving a wide variety of examples)
- Providing practice that is authentic and relevant (individualizing to student needs) (Hughes, Morris, Therrien, & Benson, 2017)

Implicit instruction is less direct, but it is still intentional. "In the case of implicit learning, learners remain unaware of the learning that has taken place, although it is evident in the behavioral responses they make" (Ellis, 2009, p. 3). The teacher knows what learning is taking place, but the children may not be aware of it.

Literacy skills are best cultivated when implicit and explicit teaching are balanced. We want you to consider how to teach those skills in the context of a children's text, as opposed to isolated, disconnected methods. We also want you to contemplate how to do this type of teaching in a developmentally appropriate way.

Principle 7

TALK ABOUT USING CHILDREN'S TEXTS TO TEACH STRATEGIES

Think about how you were taught to read and write words. Try to remember a specific moment. Did your teacher use a workbook where you practiced matching pictures to simple words? Did your mom read aloud and point out words as she read?

Now, consider the discussion between Mr. Miller, a first-grade teacher, and Mrs. Nguyen, his school's reading specialist (figure 7.1). What is similar to how you learned to decode words? What is different?

Think about what Mr. Miller (figure 7.1) is experiencing. He seeks advice from the literacy specialist Mrs. Nguyen, because he has read

Mr. Miller: My team just read studies about decoding and learned that it should include systematic, explicit instruction. We're having trouble with what that means for our teaching.

Mrs. Nguyen: Great, you're digging in research. Did you understand systematic and explicit?

Mr. Miller: We think systematic means we have well-developed plans for teaching decoding to each of our students. And, this would be done in a very direct way, like the children and I would have focused practice with specific strategies related to decoding.

Mrs. Nguyen: What will your team have to know in order to directly teach decoding?

Mr. Miller: Well, the research indicates that decoding is best learned when letters and sounds are taught in context, so we have to know ways to engage phonemic awareness, like manipulating phonemes. For sure, the 44 speech sounds and letters or letter combinations that go with those. And, word families and patterns, like CVCe. Actually, we have to know a lot!

Mrs. Nguyen: You got it. And, all of that knowledge needs to be automatic so that you can respond to individuals during explicit instruction. Do you remember what the research said about the role of meaning in this systematic, explicit decoding instruction?

Mr. Miller: This is where we are stuck. The research seems to point to authentic texts. This is different from the phonics worksheets that we have used in the past.

Mrs. Nguyen: Yes, but it can be done in the same way. The book will become your worksheet.

Mr. Miller: What do you mean?

Mrs. Nguyen: Use actual words from the text, pull them out for explicit instruction and put them back in for practice. Opportunities to teach specific decoding strategies are in the words. You systematically plan ways to directly teach those while reading with children. Scaffold in a way that allows for gradual release of using the decoding strategies.

Mr. Miller: Hmm…that will be different from how we taught before but definitely doable. Let me see if we can plan for that decoding instruction with the texts in our inventors iZone.

Figure 7.1 A little talk about systematic, explicit word learning

research that has obviously made him think about the way he instructs children in decoding. Mrs. Nguyen is proposing that he explore the authentic use of children's texts for systematic, explicit instruction, as opposed to simply relying on isolated worksheet experiences. While using children's texts to implicitly teach comprehension strategies like questioning and connecting might seem familiar to most teachers, like it was for Mr. Miller, using a children's texts to explicitly teach a code-based skill might not be as familiar.

Principle 7 provides pathways for you to follow as you become a master literacy teacher in early childhood classrooms. You will gain ideas for implementing text-based explicit and implicit instruction that is developmentally appropriate. These ideas are centered on discussions about current research regarding:

- Oral language
- Concepts about print
- Phonemic awareness
- Alphabet knowledge
- Phonics
- Fluency
- Vocabulary
- Comprehension
- Writing

USE CHILDREN'S TEXTS TO TEACH IMPORTANT LITERACY SKILLS

Master literacy teachers, like Mr. Miller, are constantly working hard to understand the science of teaching literacy, including when and how to use systematic explicit and implicit instruction. This teaching is guided by evidence-based research, practices, and assessments that have been tested repeatedly and very carefully analyzed (Stanovich & Stanovich, 2003). What better place to begin your trek to becoming a master literacy teacher than to focus on important literacy skills and the research surrounding them? As you take time to focus on each area, notice how writing can be woven into all of them.

Focus on Oral Language and Concepts about Print

In early childhood classrooms, teachers should spend much time talking with and to students and allowing them to talk to each other. However, it is not just the talk that matters; it is the type of talk that takes place. Be very purposeful in your talk with young children, being sure to:

- Ask questions that move beyond "yes" and "no" answers
- Engage in conversational talk, during systematic lessons and play, that involves more than simply giving directions
- Think aloud to model critical questions and conversations about learning
- Provide children room to inquire and explore through play, which will promote their own critical questions and conversations about learning

Oral language can easily be developed through language-rich environments and through systematic implicit instruction. A great place for this type of implicit instruction is read alouds. "When a favorite book is re-read aloud many times, the child becomes familiar with the patterns of language, expects certain things to be on certain pages, and learns when it is time to turn the page" (Wilson, 2012, p. 271).

For example, *Don't Let the Pigeon Drive the Bus* or other Pigeon tales by Mo Willems provide opportunities for the children to interact with the Pigeon. The children must be receptive to the questions and requests that the Pigeon makes and respond appropriately. A book like *Because*, also by Mo Willems, offers ample opportunities to talk deeply about how our actions have a ripple effect on others. You can even take this into writing opportunities where children think about their own *because* moments. Depending on their developmental level, they may draw, label, write sentences, or compose longer pieces. You may write in front of them as a model, share the writing as a whole class or small group, or have them engage in independent writing. The point is that writing gives you space to confer with and explicitly teach individual children, expanding both their writing and oral language skills all at the same time.

Read alouds, shared reading, and choice writing experiences provide space for children to implicitly learn concepts about print (CAP). CAP components such as book holding, beginning and ending of books/stories, and the idea that print carries meaning can all be taught implicitly through proper questioning. With a book like *The Word Collector* by Peter Reynolds, you model how to hold a book, where to begin, and where it ends. In addition, you can make special note of the many words in the images and text to highlight print and the relationship to meaning.

Shared reading and writing experiences where the teacher uses a book or text that has been enlarged (big books, poems on chart paper, books projected on Smart Boards, etc.) can also be used to dig deeper into print conventions. Just remember, read the book once for enjoyment, and then explore one or two CAP components upon subsequent reads. Teaching too many at once

I CLEKTROKS.

Figure 7.2 Emergent stage of writing

might overwhelm young children; it's better to teach one or two skills very well, rather than just brush over many skills at once.

You can use highlighter tape or Wikki Stix to mark particular print conventions as you teach, being sure to talk about their importance. With *The Word Collector*, you can use one color of highlighter tape to mark the uppercase letters in names and at the beginning of sentences. You can talk about the difference between those and other letters in the text. Then, your shared writing experience can give space for you to model and for the children to practice creating a class text that applies the use of upper- and lowercase letters. Making implicit connections between reading and writing will encourage your children to transfer what they are learning about CAP from one element of literacy to the other.

Perhaps your students independently write a response to *The Word Collector*, like a piece about their own collections or about their favorite words. You can confer with each student, asking questions about the print convention choices they make. Maybe one child writes a sentence like the one in figure 7.2 (I collect rocks.). The CAP strengths are that the child capitalizes the beginning of the sentence and uses ending punctuation. There is understanding that letters and words carry meaning. Observation would indicate left to right directionality. What is clearly missing in terms of CAP is appropriate spacing between words.

Your goal is to highlight strengths and help the child see areas of confusion and make connections to previous learning experiences that guide him in the right direction. Assessment can inform your decisions about that. Independent writing time and conferences are great ways to immediately address the needs of children. Take a look at table 7.1 to enhance your understanding of the importance of these two skills.

Focus on Phonological Awareness

Cassano (2018) defines phonological awareness (PA) as the ability to be consciously aware of the sounds of language, moving to an ability to manipulate sounds through phonemic awareness. PA is:

- A general awareness of sound (our language is made of larger blocks of sound like sentences, words, syllables, body/coda or onset/rime, rhymes)

Table 7.1 A quick look at what research says about oral language and phonological awareness development and teaching

Oral language	• Broad measures of oral reading, like growing a child's expressive (speaking) and receptive (listening) language skills, have been linked to later literacy success (Cassano, 2018). • "Print concepts are best learned implicitly in the context of examining and processing text rather than taught explicitly in isolated lessons" (Reutzel & Cooter, 2019, p. 98).
Phonological awareness	• The earliest evidence of auditory response is sixteen weeks, with significantly greater response around twenty-six weeks (Puddu & Fanos, 2012). • Syllable sound work might be easier when children play with /ka/ (the body) and /t/ (the coda) first in a one-syllable word like *cat* (Cassady & Smith, 2004; Phillips & Piasta, 2013). • "Mastery [of these phonological awareness skills] begins during the middle to end portion of kindergarten, with some children continuing to resolve these skills into first grade" (Cassady & Smith, 2004, p. 262). • Most children can master lower-level phonological awareness skills without explicit instruction, but when they are ready for work at the phoneme-level, explicit instruction is especially important for children who are struggling with sounds (Cassano, 2018; Phillips & Piasta, 2013). • "Knowledge at higher levels of [phonological awareness was] emerging in children even as they were still mastering the lower levels" (Cassano, 2018, p. 117).

- A more sophisticated awareness of sound (phonemic awareness manipulates individual sounds by isolating/matching/counting, blending, segmenting, deleting, and inserting phonemes)

PA is not:

- Phonics
- Word identification and decoding (Reutzel & Cooter, 2019)

PA is about *sound only*. Yet, it is linked closely to strategies that children use to match letters to sounds and ultimately decode (read) and encode (spell) words within a text. It is built on a continuum of skills, some more difficult for young children than others (Adams, 1990; Cassano, 2018; Reutzel & Cooter, 2019). Figure 7.3 shows the complexity of PA.

The awareness of larger units of sound is easier for children to grasp, and this learning starts at a very young age. Perhaps children even become

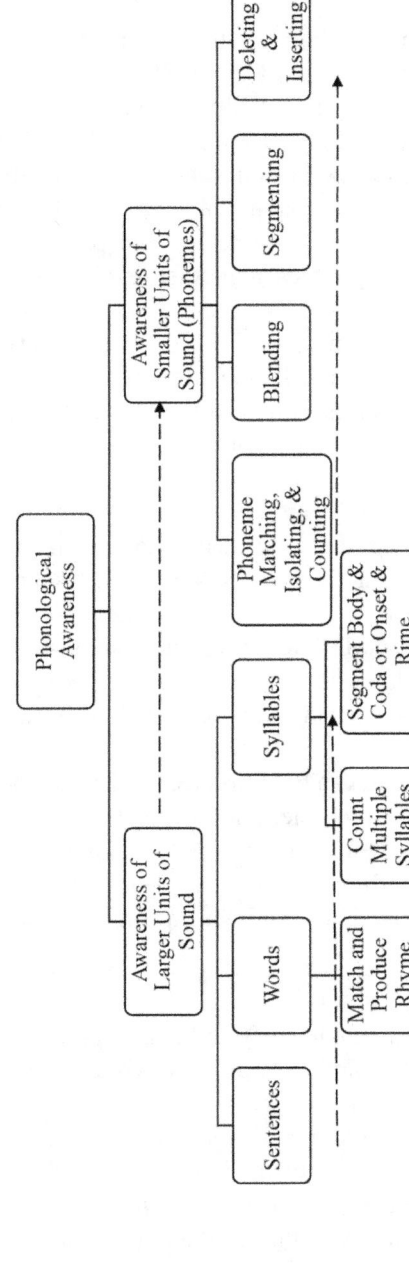

Figure 7.3 The continuum of complexity in PA

consciously aware of the idea that sentences are made of words in utero. They can hear Mom's voice and may begin to develop a conscious awareness that there is a string of sounds (sentences) followed by a short pause (the break between sentences).

From there, young children begin to hear the pauses in sentences between words and develop an awareness of words. Parents and teachers can begin to play with words, including rhyme, alliteration, and onomatopoeia through read alouds, talk, and fun songs. Reading a book like *Over in the Meadow* by Jill McDonald gives plenty of opportunity to implicitly teach beginning phonological awareness by singing and playing with rhyming words.

Children then hear the almost imperceptible pauses between syllables. They can also manipulate syllables at another level, like breaking apart:

- Onset (the consonant(s) sound up to the vowel sound) and rime (vowel sound and everything after it): /k/ and /at/ for cat
- Body (the initial consonant(s) sound and the vowel sound) and coda (everything after the vowel): /ka/ and /t/ for cat

Sheep in a Jeep by Nancy Shaw provides opportunity to explicitly explore word families (sheep, jeep, leap, etc.) using body/coda and onset/rime. Just remember, it's about reading the book first. Play with sounds as long as there is an interest, and it is fun.

Consider the difficulty when teaching phoneme-level skills (figure 7.3). For example, blending is easier than segmenting (Cassano, 2018), so once children can identify and match individual phonemes (usually initial), you might consider teaching blending. But, don't think of the continuum like a sequence or steps. Children can be introduced to harder phonemic awareness while they are still mastering easier phonological tasks.

Any text with simple words can be used to explicitly teach identifying, matching, counting blending, and segmenting. In the second sentence of *Giraffes Can't Dance* by Giles Andreae, it ends in the word *thin*, which can be:

✓ ✓ ✓
- Identified and counted: identify and count phonemes in *thin* (/th/ /i/ /n/ = 3 phonemes; the number of phonemes doesn't match the number of letters; it's about sound)
- Matched: The /th/ in *thin* is the same as the /th/ in *thick*
- Blended: starting with the individual phonemes and putting them together to make a word (/th/+/i/+/n/ = *thin*)
- Segmented: starting with the word and breaking it into the individual phonemes (*thin*=/th/+/i/+/n/)

Willoughby Wallaby Woo by Dennis Lee, and other books that purposefully manipulate phonemes, is a great text to use when planning explicit instruction for phoneme deletion and insertion. You can even add the child's own name to the phoneme manipulation pattern used in the book. For example, *Willoughby Wallaby Him, an elephant sat on Kim*.

- Deletion: remove an individual phoneme (remove /k/ to get /im/)
- Insertion/substitution: adding an individual phoneme (insert /s/ before *Kim* to get *skim*; or substitute /s/ for /k/ in *Kim* to get *sim*)

Understanding PA is hard. It is important to internalize the concept, its components, and the variation in the difficulty of those components. As we noted in principle 3, you must also know the needs of your children. When systematically teaching, it is important that you assess each child's PA skills so that you know specifically what you need to teach. Table 7.5 gives you some options for PA assessments. Once you know what explicit instruction is needed, then you can use read alouds, games, circle time, and thematic iZones to continue to implicitly play with phonological awareness.

It is important to remember that PA is just one part of a comprehensive literacy program. It works in conjunction with other pieces of literacy. But, when you teach PA in your balanced literacy program, consider:

- Development of oral language
  - Oral language skills impact phonological awareness. So, use purposeful, interactive dialogue with children.
  - Low levels of expressive (speaking) vocabulary may hinder a child's ability to learn PA skills, so move beyond simple directions or yes/no questions when working with young children.
  - Children need the ability to use decontextualized language to express abstract concepts. PA is an abstract concept, so use read alouds and shared reading experiences to help children express their understanding through playfully talking about sounds.
- Individualize systematic, explicit instruction for phonemic awareness
  - Intervention with systematic, explicit phonemic awareness instruction in kindergarten and first grade is essential for later reading success, especially for students struggling with PA. However, the effects of this instruction may be delayed until second grade, so be patient.
  - Don't try to teach more than two PA skills at the same time.
  - Keep lessons short, around five to seven minutes.

- Teach in combination with letter learning and time in print
  - The phonemic awareness instruction by itself is not enough. Combine high levels of expressive language with direct instruction of higher levels of phonemic awareness and letter/sound knowledge, all in the context of time in books and time spent in authentic, emergent writing experiences.
- Create learning experiences that are based on known student need and that are playful and fun, avoiding drill-type learning. Then, help children apply their newfound awareness to authentic reading and writing experiences (Cassano, 2018; Lonigan, Burgess, & Anthony, 2000; NELP, 2008; NICHD, 2000; Reutzel & Cooter, 2019).

Focus on Letters

Letter learning is important. But, what does letter learning actually include? Alphabetic principle includes knowing and forming the letters of the alphabet. However, it also includes identifying the sounds that those letters can make, which is letter-sound correspondence (Invernizzi & Buckrop, 2018). As you think about letter-sound correspondence, we want you to consider the importance of using authentic reading experiences for your alphabet instruction.

Alphabetic understanding is similar to what happens with PA; some letters and letter-sound combinations are easier to learn and use than others, but learning them is not necessarily lockstep. While we know this about letters, there really is no solid evidence to point us in one direction for strategies for teaching letters. Table 7.2 shows the complexity of the research related to teaching alphabetic principle.

What we do know is that letters in children's names, uppercase letters, and lowercase letters with visually identical uppercase partners are easier for young readers. We also know that letter names and the corresponding sounds are learned best with phonological awareness.

How much of the alphabetic principle should children know before entering kindergarten? Research seems to settle on eighteen uppercase, twelve to fifteen lowercase, and five letter sounds (Invernizzi & Buckrop, 2018; Piasta, Petscher, & Justice, 2012). For our youngest readers in Pre-K, just remember that they "are developing their knowledge of the alphabet letters but are unlikely to have yet mastered the corpus of letters" (Justice, Pence, Bowles, & Wiggins, 2006, p. 378). It is not until the end of kindergarten that children should master identification of all upper- and lowercase letters (Reutzel & Cooter, 2019).

Rapid automatic naming (RAN) of letters is a trend that arose from the NELP (2008) report. They reported correlational data, however, and did not

Table 7.2 A quick look at what research says about oral language development and teaching

Alphabetic principle	• "Emergent reading and writing behaviors . . . were linked to children's depth of alphabetic understanding and were actually precursors to and predictive of later reading success" (Invernizzi & Buckrop, 2018, p. 90).
	• Four-year-old children were only moderately more likely to know uppercase letters when the letter name is in the pronunciation, the letters appear earlier in the alphabet, or the letters correspond to phonemes learned first (Justice, Pence, Bowles, and Wiggins, 2006).
	• Children were eleven times more likely to know the first letter of their names, exclusive to uppercase only (Pence, Turnbull, Bowles, Skibbe, Justice, & Wiggins, 2010).
	• Preschool children know more uppercase letters than lowercase, with the one exception of *i* (Pence Turnbull, Bowles, Skibbe, Justice, & Wiggins, 2010).
	• Children see more uppercase letters in environmental print, so learning uppercase is easier (Worden & Boettcher, 1990).
	• There is a greater likelihood of learning lowercase letters if the uppercase is known first because so many upper- and lowercase letters share exact structure (Pence Turnbull, Bowles, Skibbe, Justice, & Wiggins, 2010).
	• It is important to learn lowercase letters because children need that knowledge to read texts that are predominantly lowercase (Schickedanz & Collins, 2013).
	• Some researchers have found that frequency of lowercase letters in print alone does not benefit lowercase knowledge (Pence Turnbull, Bowles, Skibbe, Justice, & Wiggins, 2010).
	• There is no evidence that learning letter names before sounds is better (Ellefson, Treiman, & Kessler, 2009).
	• Learning letter names and sound correspondence with phonological awareness, however, has positive effects on letter name knowledge and fluency (Piasta & Wagner, 2010).
	• Children should know their letters without hesitation by the end of kindergarten, about one letter every two seconds or so (Reutzel & Cooter, 2019).
	• "Children who already know letters, numbers, colors, and so on tend to be able to name them quickly, but they did not learn the letters, numbers, and colors simply by being asked to name them quickly. There is simply no research that concludes that practicing things like [rapid automatic naming] improves literacy outcomes" (Paciga, Hoffman, & Teale, 2011, p. 55).

indicate that *teaching* children to say letters as fast as they can results in greater effects on reading ability. It's likely more about automaticity than anything related to speed, and it may be something that happens in conjunction with learning other early literacy skills. So, what can we take away from the research that applies easily to our teaching?

⚠ **Avoid spending explicit instructional time on letters children can learn easily. Two examples:**

- If a child easily learns the first letter of his name, along with other letters in his name, then your explicit instruction will not be focused on those letters for him. Let his name be a part of the playful implicit learning that takes place.
- If there are fifteen uppercase letters that visually correspond to their lowercase partners, then you will not explicitly teach those fifteen lowercase letters. Let the children lead the discoveries about those similarities.

⚠ **Avoid teaching the same letter to all students at one time**

- Let assessment be your guide to explicit alphabetic principle instruction. There is great variety in when and how young children learn letter names, shapes, and sound correspondence, so targeted explicit instruction on the *harder-to-learn* letters is best.
- Focus on two or three letters at a time so that children can analyze similarities and differences.

⚠ **Avoid neglecting higher-level reading skills (vocabulary and comprehension) at the expense of spending too much class time on learning letters and sounds.**

- There are "strengthening associations between letter-sound knowledge, phonological awareness, and invented spelling as children get closer to actual reading" (Invernizzi & Buckrop, 2018, p. 97).

⚠ **Avoid relying only on isolated alphabet practice**

- Use explicit instruction but know that application is a must as well; research supports the idea that effective instruction "intentionally links letter names to phonemes in print" (Invernizzi & Buckrop, 2018, p. 101).
- "Use multifaceted approaches that take into account the child, letter, and environmental characteristics" (Invernizzi & Buckrop, 2018, p. 100).

Think about the book *Silly Sally* by Audrey Wood. It would be easy to use this text to teach oral language, concepts about print, phonemic awareness, and alphabetic principle all at the same time in a shared reading experience with a small group of children. The work with this book could be a place where the teacher "compares and contrasts features of letters and connects alphabet learning with print concepts, phonological awareness, and writing" (Invernizzi & Buckrop, 2018, p. 105). And, *all* of it is done in the context of authentic literature.

Let's say that you have assessed the small group of children and determined that they need to know the /th/ sound in the diagraph TH and the /n/ sound in N, as well as differences between upper- and lowercase letters. You can systematically use the book to implicitly expand oral language by having the children chorally read some parts of the text and engage in discussion about whether or not someone could walk to town on their hands while sleeping. Implicitly, you can strengthen phonological awareness because of the rhyme in the book.

Explicitly, you can draw the children's attention to the upper- and lowercase uses of the letter *N* (which occur in the beginning, middle, and end of multiple words); have the children say the letter name and sound, write the letters together to focus on upper- and lowercase differences, read the words with the letter *N* in the text, and write a few other words that start with *N* for their Words I Know boxes (or any other place where children collect letters and words).

You can then focus on the more difficult letters of *TH*, which form a digraph. Have the children talk about how two letters make one sound, say the sound, write some simple words like *the* and *they* from the text, and then have the children suggest some other TH words for the Words I Know boxes. These words in the box can be read later and used in writing. Importantly, they celebrate and highlight learning.

As we have discussed throughout this book, each reader has different needs, and this is no different for alphabetic principle. Since there is no consistent, research-based support for the order in which to teach letter names and there is variation in which letters young readers learn first (Justice, Pence, Bowles, & Wiggins, 2006; Reutzel & Cooter, 2019), teachers should first assess student letter knowledge and develop a plan for teaching letter names, shapes, and sounds based on the needs of the individual child. See figure 7.5 for a few assessments that are easy to administer.

Focus on Fluent Decoding and Word Recognition

Now that you have a good foundation for oral language, print conventions, phonological awareness, and alphabetic principle, let's put those together to help readers develop more reading skills and strategies. Decoding strategies can be used to learn *phonics*. Fluency has three interconnected parts (accuracy, automaticity, and prosody), which can be partially developed through decoding strategies (Rasinski, Reutzel, Chard, & Linan-Thompson, 2011). Word recognition strategies help readers apply meaning to the words that are decoded and read fluently. Meaning, of course, should always be a focus, even when learning code-based skills, like phonics.

While it sounds simple when broken down, fluent decoding that also focuses on meaning requires complex strategies. Readers must:

- Attend to letter and sound correspondence, including blends, digraph, trigraphs, diphthongs, schwas, and r-Controlled vowels
  - Start this attention with the first letter/sound of words, which are easier for emerging readers, and move to ending and medial letter/sound, which are harder
- Take words apart, including body/coda and onset/rime
- Learn high frequency words
- Learn to repeat/reread when it doesn't make sense
  - Syntax (grammar)—Does it sound right?
  - Meaning—Does it make sense?
  - Visual—Does it look like what I said?
- Take longer words apart, including syllables, prefixes, suffixes, roots/bases
- Link the unknown to the known (schema for words)
- Focus on meaning (schema for the context) (Clay, 2005; Fountas & Pinnell, 2017; Reutzel & Cooter, 2019)

There is certainly a lot for a young reader to process, but do not be overwhelmed by all that you must teach. And, remember that teaching phonics and word recognition should not be at the expense of lots of systematic, authentic reading and writing experiences.

Isn't it interesting to think about daily writing as essential for learning phonics and word recognition? Children can apply what they learn about decoding to encoding (spelling) and word recognition. It is important to connect what your children are learning in books to writing experiences as well.

Another consideration when teaching these strategies is that instruction should be with authentic texts (limiting decodable, contrived texts). While our first inclination may be to reach for those contrived texts that are specifically designed to focus on a particular phonics skill, much research (see table 7.3) points to exposure to authentic print as a key factor in reading development; this is why we devoted principle 2 to classroom libraries, chapter 4 to the use of literacy in play, chapter 5 to read alouds, and chapter 6 to learning content through literacy.

Much can be learned through engagement with authentic texts and well-planned implicit instruction, but sometimes explicit instruction is needed. Both Fountas and Pinnell (2017) and Bear, Invernizzi, Templeton, and Johnston (2016) have programs for explicit decoding/encoding instruction that many school districts use.

Table 7.3 A quick look at what research says about phonics development and teaching

Decoding, encoding, and word recognition fluency (phonics)	• Effective teachers can teach phonics and word recognition strategies and still ensure that children are "consistently reading more challenging books, writing more coherent pieces, and exhibiting the highest levels of engagement" (Wharton-McDonald, 2018, p. 151). • Writing leaves deeper memory traces than letter/word recognition alone (Reutzel & Cooter, 2019). • In her review of a pivotal study conducted by David Share in 1995, Wharton-McDonald (2018) ascertained that, "when the reader is immersed in 'natural texts. . .,' there will be many words that are familiar based on their high-frequency occurrences and a smaller number of words that will require the more resource-draining recoding process" (p. 154). • While phonetically regular words do appear in contrived texts, sometimes the quest to make all words easily decodable is at the expense of meaning, confusing young readers (Mesmer, Cunningham, & Hiebert, 2012). • In her review of a pivotal study conducted by Keith Stanovich in 1980, Wharton-McDonald (2018) found that "skilled readers demonstrate automaticity in the service of higher-order comprehension" (p. 155), essentially disavowing the use of word lists for reading evaluation.

Table 7.4 A Quick look at what research says about vocabulary, comprehension, and prosodic fluency

Vocabulary, comprehension, and prosodic fluency	Goldstein and Randolph (2017) indicate that "teachers should base the facilitation of vocabulary on the developmental appropriateness for the individual child and naturally occurring opportunities during activities and interactions" (p. 71). A synthesis of research shows that effective readers "use strategies that help them retain, organize, and evaluate the information they are reading." These include concept and story mapping, questioning (both asking and answering), summarizing, visualizing, connecting to background knowledge, knowing text patterns/structures, identifying and depicting ideas and relationships, and monitoring for understanding (Snow & RAND, 2002, p. 32). "Engaging students in various forms of reading practice that results in performing readings of texts for an audience is inherently motivating and effective in promoting reading fluency" (Rasinksi, Reutzel, Chard, & Linan-Thompson, 2011, p. 305).

These can be effective components of your balanced literacy program: reading aloud, shared/guided reading/writing experiences, and independent reading/writing that balance code-based with meaning-based skills (NICHD, 2000; NELP, 2008; Reutzel & Cooter, 2019; Wharton-McDonald, 2018). This means that explicit phonics instruction is just one part of what we do as early childhood teachers. And, there is no single method of explicit instruction that is more effective than another (Reutzel & Cooter, 2019).

Before teaching fluent decoding/encoding and word recognition, get to know your readers and writers very well. Watch them read, and assess their ability to fluently decode/encode and ascribe meaning to texts. Table 7.5 offers a variety of possibilities when it comes to assessing decoding/encoding and word recognition.

One assessment, in particular, is Running Records (Clay, 2005). With this, you can clearly note and analyze the accuracy of a child's reading. This is something that can be done at any time in any classroom of early readers; all you need is a child, a book, a piece of paper, and a pencil.

Miscue Analysis (Cooter, Flynt, & Cooter, 2014) is easier to use with readers who are moving into more proficiency since Running Records become difficult to obtain when a reader develops an adequate level of speed while reading. You just cannot write that fast. The importance of these two assessments is that you are actually watching a reader in action, instead

Table 7.5 Assessments appropriate for early literacy

Assessment	Skill
Avoid the One-Size-Fits-All Approach by Using Assessment	
Ekwall/Shanker Reading Inventory (Shanker & Cockrum, 2019)	Phonological Awareness, Letter Naming, Sight Words, Phonics/Decoding, Reading/Listening Word Recognition & Comprehension (Levels)
Yopp Singer Test of Phoneme Segmentation (Yopp, 1995)	Phonological Awareness
An Observation Survey of Early Literacy Achievement (3rd ed.) (Clay, 2005)	Concepts About Print, Letter Naming, Decoding/Word Recognition/Fluency (Levels), Writing
Flynt/Cooter Comprehensive Reading Inventory-2 Assessment for K-12 Reading Skills in English & Spanish (2nd ed.). (Cooter, Flynt, & Cooter, 2014)	Phonemic Awareness, Alphabet Awareness/Letter Naming, High Frequency Words, Phonics/Decoding, Oral Word Recognition/Fluency/Silent Comprehension (Levels)
Words Their Way: Word Study for Phonics, Vocabulary, and Spelling Instruction (6th ed.). (Bear, Invernizzi, Templeton, & Johnston, 2016)	Encoding (Spelling Levels)

of just utilizing a computer-based reading assessment that only gives final results.

Teaching fluent decoding/encoding and word recognition does not have to be complicated or controversial. Just understand that:

- Both implicit and explicit instruction for individual students is vital, and this instruction must be systematic (planned purposefully)
- Readers use both bottom-up and top-down approaches to reading new words, so teaching should be balanced, focusing on both code-based and meaning-based practice throughout the day
- Sounds, letters, and meaning all work together within context to enhance fluent decoding and encoding; it is not one over the other
- Context dependency for decoding is normal in beginning reading, but the goal is to move toward automaticity and systematic strategy use; context with fluent readers is about comprehension, not about decoding
- Teach with authentic reading and writing experiences (modeled, shared, guided, and independent)

Let's think about what this might look like. Perhaps you have a small group of children in your first-grade class who is struggling with vowel digraph. You, of course, will provide much exposure to read alouds and modeled writing where you implicitly teach reading and writing fluently; you may even briefly note words with vowel digraphs. You also plan for explicit instruction through shared reading and guided reading experiences where children practice fluent reading and study words with vowel digraphs.

For example, you could read *Miss Spider's Tea Party* by David Kirk as a read aloud. After the read aloud, you might tell the children that you were fascinated by two words in the book and briefly introduce the digraphs of *ea* and *ee* by writing *tea* and *bee* on paper, saying the sounds, reading the words, and talking about these vowel digraphs. The children might want to add some words that they know or saw in the book to your list as well.

On another day, ask the children to reread Kirk's book along with you in a choral, shared reading experience, stopping to use highlighter tape to mark words (*tea, leaves, meal, beetle, three, bee*, etc.) with the vowel digraphs of *ea* and *ee*, ensuring that meaning is addressed. Talk about the letter teams again and the sounds that they make in each word, allowing the children to explore and make discoveries about these words and others found in the text. After reading, have the children help you add to your list that you started previously, talking about the importance of looking for and analyzing these and other vowel combinations in words.

From there, you would plan guided reading experiences where these students can practice fluency by applying their awareness of these digraphs and begin to investigate other vowel digraph. Look for *authentic* texts that provide these opportunities and are within the children's zone of proximal development. Remember, the authenticity of a text will ensure the meaning connections are available. Guided reading also has built-in time for word work, so children can engage in word sort activities (Bear, Invernizzi, Templeton, & Johnston, 2016).

In addition, as you confer with children during their independent reading and writing, you would be sure to ask whether or not they encountered any diagraphs in texts, either learned or new, that they can use to assist with decoding. You can also assist them as they apply what they learned about vowel digraphs to their writing. Just remember, there is a "slant of development" for reading and writing; children can often apply a particular decoding strategy to reading before they can apply it to encoding in their writing (Bear, Invernizzi, Templeton, & Johnston, 2016).

While schools spend a large portion of their budgets on programs that provide isolated, worksheet-type activities for phonics and word identification instruction, there is no need for this waste of resources. Systematic instruction that uses authentic texts in the confines of balanced literacy is all that is needed. The idea is that you are helping children to become strategic readers, while at the same time explicitly teaching them phonics and word identification skills. And, you are giving children plenty of opportunity to apply and extend those strategies to other phonics skills.

Consider Fluency, Vocabulary, and Comprehension
Even Further

While we have talked previously about the importance of meaning, take a little more time to think about vocabulary, comprehension, and the prosodic side of fluency (inflection, tone, pace, character voices, etc.). These higher-level reading skills are closely intertwined because they are essential for making meaning.

Meaning is not something that can be given to a reader in one cohesive chunk; it has to be strategically constructed from many pieces (Snow & RAND, 2002). Readers must have strategies to have a *transaction* with the text (Rosenblatt, 1994). Those strategies might include: monitoring comprehension, activating and connecting background knowledge, visualizing and inferring, determining importance, and summarizing and synthesizing (Harvey & Goudvis, 2017). Readers and writers must also develop expertise with vocabulary and prosodic fluency.

When young readers seek to draw meaning from a text or convey meaning in their writing, they knit these comprehension strategies with vocabulary and fluency usage. While we may highlight the prosody of fluency or the strategy of making connections in a model, it is important to remember that all three parts of fluency and all of the reading strategies are used in chorus by readers. The good news is that "we can teach all of these [meaning-making] strategies in developmentally appropriate ways to kids at all grade levels" (Harvey & Goudvis, 2017, p. 23).

Read alouds provide the perfect opportunities for teachers to help children build vocabulary, prosodic fluency, and comprehension skills in meaningful ways. These "heightened searches for meaning" occur when a teacher thoughtfully selects books with unexpected formats, plots, or story elements (Roser, 2012, p. 409).

Once again, the importance of being an avid reader and knowing children's texts cannot be underestimated. When reading children's texts, you will want to read with the eye of a teacher. In other words, you make note of books that use language that exemplifies the use of the perfect words (see Principles 1 and 5 for some examples of texts with this quality). This, in turn, will allow your young readers and writers to extend their own understanding. You will want to push vocabulary learning beyond simple word learning because that does not appear to link to later reading success (NELP, 2008).

For example, *Chrysanthemum* by Kevin Henkes provides examples for dynamic vocabulary learning:

- *Just right* words: "Chrysanthemum wilted"—a beautiful, poetic way to say that someone whose name is also a flower's name felt defeated and depressed
- Words to explore and use in speaking, reading, and writing: absolutely, miserably, scarcely, pish, precious, priceless, fascinating, and much more

As a teacher who values vocabulary instruction, you want your young readers and writers to be able to infer meaning while reading and to be able to use *just right* and varied vocabulary in their writing and speaking. When you read aloud *Chrysanthemum*, you will want to stop to rave about the way that Henkes uses *wilted*. Engage your young readers in this very important moment.

- "Oh, I love the way that Henkes says, 'Chrysanthemum wilted.' Do you know what wilted means? What was happening in the story to make Chrysanthemum feel this way? Why didn't Henkes just say that Chrysanthemum felt sad? Isn't he brilliant? I want to be able to write like him."

With a few open questions, you can allow children to inquire about words, meaning, and the beauty of a writer's craft.

When you model writing, try to imitate Henkes' use of figurative language. You might write something like, "Sunshine burned with anger when her brother revealed her biggest secret." When you confer with writers during independent writing, look for opportunities to encourage them to do the same.

Reading experiences will also prompt word collection. Chrysanthemum's mom says, "Oh, pish . . . Your name is beautiful." Thinking aloud during the read aloud can show children how you should be curious about words that you do not know, try to use context to determine meaning, and sometimes look outside of the text to define complex vocabulary.

- You might say, "*Pish*, I don't know what that word means. Let me see. Does it tell me here in the text? Not really. Is it like a word I know? Not really. I know *wish*, but that doesn't make sense here. Maybe I will have to look this one up."

Take the dialog from Chrysanthemum's mom even further by thinking aloud about meaning. Wonder aloud about what they are implying by questioning, making connections, and inferring. It might sound like this, "I wonder what Chrysanthemum's parents are trying to say to her. They seem to not listen to her worries. I think her parents were trying to encourage her and tell her that she shouldn't worry. I've done that with my kids before. Have your parents ever tried to help you not worry?"

You can then take it a bit further to practice prosody by saying, "Now, that I know that they don't want her to worry, I can reread this sentence like this. Pish (exaggerating the sound and waving your hand in the air), your name is *beautiful* (emphasizing the last word)."

Supported and independent reading experiences provide opportunities for children to learn to recognize when they struggle with meaning. While guiding reading and writing experiences and conferring, you can easily and explicitly individualize instruction, asking students probing questions about meaning, guiding them to attend to strategies when meaning breaks down, and encouraging them to focus on prosody.

There are plenty of opportunities in these situations to model and support readers as they put these complex skills into practice. When engaging in read alouds, modeled writing, and shared reading/writing, be sure that they know that readers and writers:

- Make connections to life (self and others) and texts previously read
- Ask questions before, during, and after reading; they should also know that curious readers search for answers, even if they cannot be found in the text
- Infer and visualize what an author might mean and make predictions about what might happen. Note: this takes much skill because it requires the

reader to connect what is known (schema) to text evidence to determine what the author meant, but did not specifically say; if a child is only five or six, she doesn't have a lot of schema stored for that yet
- Attend to text features like illustrations, captions, and graphics and know when and how to use them with the text
- Notice punctuation, bold print, and other crafty features that authors use that enhance meaning and guide prosodic fluency
- Know when something does not make sense or sound right (aurally or silently inside of the reader's head), and then reread, drawing on the above to clarify the confusion
- Summarize and synthesize information read; for younger children, it is helpful to teach them to do this in smaller chunks rather than wait until the end of a text

Once again, the strategies that readers must use in order to fully comprehend or read with prosody are dense. Writers have to think about this when composing a text too. It is all beautifully entangled. Remember what NAEYC (2009) tells us.

Children need regular and active interactions with print. . . . Experiences in these early years begin to define the assumptions and expectations about becoming literate and give children the motivation to work toward learning to read and write. From these experiences children learn that reading and writing are valuable tools that will help them do many things in life. (p. 3)

PUT IT ALL TOGETHER AND KEEP LEARNING

As a teacher of young children, there is so much that you have to know and do to develop literacy skills. Remember, everything you need to teach literacy can be found in children's texts. All you have to do is utilize the texts with intention and purpose. Shannon Mitrisin, a kindergarten teacher, puts together many of the strategies and skills talked about in this principle. She cultivates literacy skills with children's texts and balanced instruction (figure 7.4).

This chapter ends where it began. It is a circular story of sorts. We asked that you be very purposeful with the instructional decisions that you make about these very important literacy skills. We proposed that you know the research that supports what you do and then we showed you what that can look like in practice using children's texts as your basis. Now, we ask you to come back to research one more time. Just like you would not settle on one report or one study to guide your teaching, don't settle on only what chapter 7 presents. Once you finish this book, please dig deeper into these concepts

 Spotlight on Practice

Shannon Mitrisin

Kindergarten Teacher

Interactive read alouds are my passion! I enjoy seeing my students react to text, and illustrations. It's powerful to see my students take on the same text features in their own writing. Typically we spend a week on a specific title. We work as a class family to dissect the text and attempt to understand why the author and illustrator did certain things to tell (or show) the story.

We always begin the week listening to the whole text for the sole purpose of enjoyment. Throughout the week we reread the story and follow it up with a comprehension skill using depth and complexity. For example: retelling, sequencing, taking on the perspective of the characters, locating patterns in a text...etc. There is whole-group interaction with lots of time to turn and talk to allow for dialogue about the story.

Most of the time I will use the read aloud text to carry over into writer's workshop. I model writing part of what was observed in the read aloud (authors craft) to invite students to try it as authors when they write. They merge the minilesson idea into their writing. I want them to know they are authors and illustrators just like the ones from the books we are reading.

During conferring, I take the time to push my writers individually, based on their writing level. I might say, "I notice your character is talking." When authors want to show someone is talking in their story, they use quotation marks. Would you like to try that too?

Guided reading offers a smaller setting to work on reading strategies and decoding, based on the group's reading level. We work on comprehension and reading to make meaning. For example, if one of my readers pauses after reading a sentence or word, I might comment, "I noticed that you paused after reading the sentence. Tell me why. What did you notice?" This reinforces to the reader that what was initially read may not have made sense. They paused, went back, re-read and this time, identified their error. By asking them to state why they paused, it builds comprehension and affirms proper reading strategies.

In shared reading, we work together to identify components of a sentence and focus on specific skills using big books. The teaching focus is specific and tailored to the needs of my learners and where I need to get them to in order to be successful readers and writers.

Children's literature is a vessel to any and every lesson, content area, and/or learning standard! Anything and everything can be taught through children's literature, and I love that.

Figure 7.4 Spotlight on practice: Shannon Mitrisin, kindergarten teacher

about systematic, early literacy instruction. Like we do here, you will want to take a look at the ongoing research related to early literacy skills. Here are some places to start:

- National Association for the Education of Young Children (NAEYC) https://www.naeyc.org/
- International Literacy Association (ILA) https://www.literacyworldwide.org/
- What Works Clearinghouse (WWC) https://ies.ed.gov/ncee/wwc/

Principle 8

Connect Literacy Learning with a Reimagined Literacy Workshop

In this book, we have presented seven principles about teaching early literacy for you to consider. Within each principle, there are lots of actions to contemplate, try, and implement in your classroom. You have learned how to avoid one-sized teaching. You are well on your way to becoming a master literacy teacher of young children. In this principle, we want to provide you with picture of how the ideas from the book come together daily in your classroom and shake things up a bit. So, the information might be familiar to you with an added twist. Let's start by activating your schema. In this principle, you will learn how to:

- Implement literacy workshop
  - Define the traditional literacy workshop
  - Read and write every day with children
  - Balance literacy instruction within the workshop
  - Release literacy learning gradually

- Reimagine an integrated workshop with Literacy Exploration Opportunities (LEO)
  - Add iZones to the Balanced Literacy Diet
  - Think Literacy Exploration Opportunities (LEO): An Integrated Workshop
  - Go for it: Start a LEO-led classroom

A LITTLE TALK ABOUT GUIDING READING THEMATICALLY

In figure 8.1, two first-grade teachers, Sarah and Joan, discuss the balance between inquiry and systematic instruction that takes place when teachers include iZones as a central part of classroom learning. Here, they are beginning to rethink their ideas about how to integrate books for guiding reading with iZone themes. As you read, consider how their questions might reflect those that you have been pondering while reading this book.

While leveling books for small group instruction that also aligns with a learning theme will take time, it will be time well spent. In addition, investigating resources that offer levels for authentic trade books will be worth your effort. This type of purposeful selection of texts used in small group, systematic reading experiences helps children gain greater connections with content while they are learning and applying literacy skills. It is more purposeful than having small group reading instruction that is disconnected from thematic learning.

Sarah: If I'm teaching in an iZone, how will I ever guide my reading groups?

Joan: Well, if iZones are the center of learning in your classroom, what if your reading groups were just an extension of that? Couldn't you make systematic, explicit instruction purposeful by extending the topics from the iZone into small groups? This might help children make practical connections as they read.

Sarah: That makes sense, but how do I find leveled books to match the themes of the iZone?

Joan: Well, I heard Scholastic Book Clubs has leveled books that fit with authentic themes. I also know that they have an app. called Scholastic Book Wizard that scans the barcode of the book to get a level. And, we can get access to the Fountas and Pinnell Leveled Books Website for a low cost. They have an online library that provides the levels of almost 70,000 books.

Sarah: Oh yeah, I remember. Fountas and Pinnell offer guidelines on leveling books yourself. This means we could level any book we choose for reading groups. That way we can choose from a larger variety of books and not just those that are already leveled.

Joan: Let's get started first by finding books in the school's leveled book library that match the iZone theme. Then, we can level the books we already have in our classrooms that are related to the theme. We can use them to guide reading with purpose.

Figure 8.1 A little talk about guiding reading thematically

It may seem an impossible task to utilize a literacy workshop to teach explicitly while concentrating on a play-based, thematic curriculum. However, this principle will put that assumption to rest. By placing the needs of the children first, we ensure early childhood classrooms that facilitate learning and empower children with the tools they need to transfer knowledge in any situation.

IMPLEMENT LITERACY WORKSHOP

Define the Traditional Literacy Workshop

"Based on the principles of time, choice, response, and community, a workshop format allows for in-depth teaching and learning, flexibility, differentiation, and ultimately, independence" (Miller, 2013, p. 11). This is the type of literacy workshop that grew out of the work of such researchers as Atwell (1987), Calkins (1994), Graves (1983), and Meyer (2010). It has been found to improve motivation and comprehension (Swift, 1993). With reading and writing workshop, children learn to:

- Feel comfortable with books and their own writing
- Choose appropriate books that "fit"
- Write based on choice
- Confer about and share books and writing
- Write in notebooks about what they are reading
- Learn strategies and skills in minilessons
- Lead book talks and publish writing

A literacy workshop allows for time to independently read and write and to share learning with others. Teachers scaffold this independent work with minilessons and important conferring sessions, gradually releasing the responsibility for learning. This, particularly, allows for many opportunities to assess individual children and teach them, both in the moment and in later systematically planned experiences. Depending on need, the workshop model (table 8.1) is organic, providing the teacher flexibility to decide where more time is needed: modeling, systematically teaching, conferring, or sharing.

The workshop offers a differentiated curriculum that allows children both cooperative and individual times for learning. Children have choice in their reading and writing and connect information as they immerse themselves in natural literacy experiences. "Workshop products provide strong and authentic evidence of learning" (Oszakiweski & Spelman, 2011, p. 25).

Table 8.1 Teaching with the workshop model

What is the structure of the workshop?	How do teachers and students interact in a workshop?	Can code-based skills fit in a workshop?
Minilesson/Mid-workshop Teaching	Modeling Reading & Writing: The teacher has the responsibility for reading/writing and engages in think-alouds to show sustained reading/writing and strategy application.	Implicit/Explicit Word Work
Minilesson/Mid-workshop Teaching	Shared Reading & Writing: The teacher has most of the responsibility for reading/writing, but the children are reading/writing with the teacher.	Implicit/Explicit Word Work
Conferring/Small Group Work	Guiding Reading & Writing or Group Reading & Writing (reading/writing clubs as example): Children work with partners or groups on reading and writing, and the teacher supports their work. The children have most of the responsibility for reading/writing.	Explicit Word Work
Independent Work/Conferring/Sharing	Independent Reading & Writing: Children have the responsibility for reading/writing. The teacher confers with them as they work on reading and writing strategies independently.	Explicit Word Work

Calkins & Teachers College Reading and Writing Project (TCWRP), n.d.; Pearson & Gallagher, 1983

Read and Write Every Day with Children

Start reading and writing with children the first week of school and continue every day. As we mentioned in principle 5, there are many benefits to reading aloud, and those include writing too. Encourage your children to read and write for themselves as well. Krashen (2004) determined that reading freely impacted children's "reading comprehension ability, writing style, vocabulary, grammar, and spelling" (p. 37). "Writing, like running or reading, is a skill that develops with use. Writers need time to write. In too many schools, this time is compromised" (Calkins & Ehrenworth, 2016, p. 8).

Because worksheets and direct instruction have taken up much time in some classrooms, children are spending less time reading and writing. These direct methods of teaching appear to be easy and make life simpler in terms of planning, but how do these teaching materials help promote connection of knowledge for the children?

In reality, they don't help. They are inadequate, and they take away from independent reading and writing time. This is important because studies have shown that children in the United States spend only about four to five minutes reading books outside of school (Anderson, Wilson, & Fielding, 1988). A study that looked at how much writing children do across three content areas, showed that they only produce 1.6 papers per week (Applebee & Langer, 2011). This is staggering. It is imperative that you immerse children in reading and writing every day.

Balance Literacy Instruction Within the Workshop

Teachers who utilize literacy workshop follow a balanced literacy approach to teaching. This includes a balance of both: teaching focus and methods.

Some teachers who do not use a balanced model might focus solely on code-based literacy skills, which follows the bottom-up approach. The belief is that young children will learn to read quickly through a heavy focus on code-based instruction. But, this does little to connect meaning for young children until after they have mastered the code. Others who do not use balanced literacy might favor a meaning-based literacy approach. Here, teachers concentrate on a top-down approach, with little explicit connection to code-based literacy skills provided.

If we truly want children to succeed, we need to ensure they are given both specific, code-based and meaning-based literacy skills and strategies all at the same time. When introduced naturally in a workshop, minilessons and small group or independent conference sessions ensure that literacy skills and strategies are systematically balanced, working together to connect information in the most relevant way. Most importantly, children are able to apply both code-based and meaning-based strategies while independently reading and writing.

Kecia Pilant, a first-grade teacher, uses a balanced literacy approach in her classroom. In figure 8.2, Kecia discusses how reading and writing workshop are implemented in her classroom. How is she balancing literacy skills in her workshop? Can you see some of the elements of a traditional workshop represented?

Think about your own approach to reading and writing in the classroom. Have you noticed your approach leans more toward top or bottom? How are you ensuring that your literacy teaching is balanced and working together to improve knowledge in your classroom? Look at figure 8.3 for a snapshot of a balanced literacy approach. Let it be your guide as you rethink balancing literacy instruction within your workshop.

Release Literacy Learning Gradually

Literacy can also be balanced through the components of a gradual release model (see table 8.1). It includes a thoughtful process of teacher- and

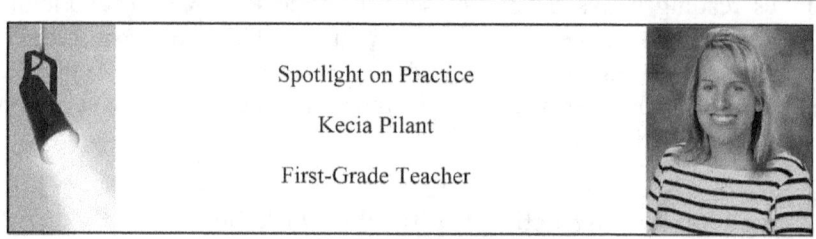

Spotlight on Practice

Kecia Pilant

First-Grade Teacher

I have a reputation as someone who grows children. Kids might grow some with basal readers and worksheets, but not as much as they will in a workshop. I use a workshop approach every day. My students leave first grade loving reading and writing.

We have book talks, which gets kids excited about the books. I search blogs, Instagram, and am constantly looking for and researching new books. The way I read aloud is animated. I use picture books for everything; it is a great way to get kids interested.

We give kids lots of choice in terms of what they write and even how they write it. We have lots of blank booklets and all different materials to use to create books. The children get to take the books that they make to our local, public library where they are put on display.

Kids won't improve if they are not writing. It is amazing how much kids can grow. I love all of my students, and I encourage them as writers.

We challenge them to try to include the minilesson component somewhere in their writing and independent reading. They give me a thumbs up when they have done it. We have some reading stations and make lots of anchor charts. I don't do worksheets.

I have to explain my approach to parents so that they won't expect to see a lot of worksheets coming home. I take a lot of pictures and share them on a class webpage so that parents see the work that is happening every day. The pictures actually serve as a great conversation starter for the kids and parents at home.

I also have a weekly newsletter that explains what they are doing in class. I show and explain their journaling and the learning notebooks that we keep. It really is an "aha" moment for them when they see the work as it is progressing.

Make sure you are the kind of teacher you want your own children to have. I'm a learner; I never stop learning. Have fun. Build relationships.

Figure 8.2 Spotlight on practice: Kecia Pilant, first-grade teacher

student-led interactions, scaffolded learning experiences, and individualized instruction. Within a literacy workshop, you will see:

- Modeling
    - Read aloud through interactive read alouds and minilessons: Show children how readers comprehend, apply fluency, decipher the meaning of unknown words, decode unknown words, attend to the text, and so on.

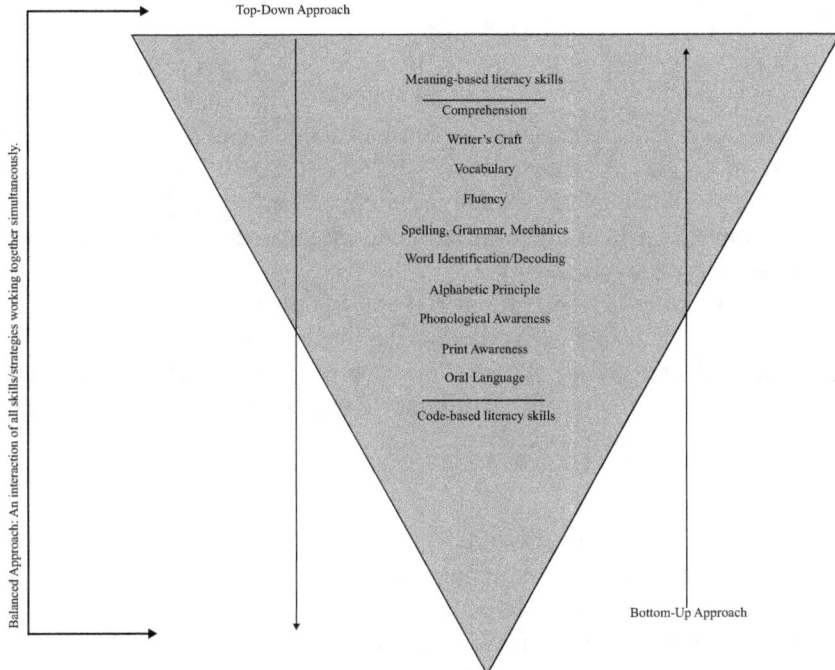

Figure 8.3   Approaches to literacy instruction

- Write aloud through interactive write alouds and minilessons: Write in front of children or share writing (yours, children's texts, children's writing) to help writers develop topics for writing, clarify confusions, add *just right* words at the right time, add or delete words, sentences, or paragraphs, edit, and so on.
- Sharing
  - Share reading: Teachers use minilessons to share big books with young children or a common class text (copies or on a smart board/projector). The teacher models the reading skills and strategies and does most of the reading, but she will ask the children to join her in the reading experience, allowing them to practice with assistance.
  - Share writing: Teachers use minilessons to engage in writing experiences where they model writing process, craft, and strategies for children. The teacher does most of the writing, but she will ask the children to join her in the writing experience, allowing for practice with assistance.

- Guiding
  - Guide reading: In small group and one-to-one guided teaching, children read carefully selected texts (sometimes on their instructional reading level) to practice independently but with some support from the teacher, like in Guided Reading (Fountas & Pinnell, 2017). When children are engaged in literacy circles, the teacher may listen to children talk about reading experiences and/or offer feedback through a reading conference or activity (Daniels, 2002).
  - Guide writing: In small groups and one-to-one guided teaching, children write and the teacher provides minilessons related to writing, providing independent practice but with some support from the teacher. The teacher may listen as the writing is produced and/or offer feedback through a writing conference or activity.
- Independent work
  - Independent reading: Children read self-selected texts individually to practice reading skills and strategies. The reader engages with the teacher and peers in reading conferences.
  - Independent writing: Children individually write self-selected pieces to practice writing skills and strategies. The writer engages with the teacher and peers in writing conferences.

This process is carefully implemented by the teacher in a continuous manner as she observes and facilitates work with children based upon their individual needs. As the children grow more knowledgeable, the teacher lets them become responsible for utilizing strategies independently. A literacy workshop emphasizes children working together and learning through balanced literacy approaches. It highlights the importance of balanced, intentional literacy instruction. We would also like to ensure that teachers are balancing their reading and writing instruction through the most natural way: integration.

REIMAGINE AN INTEGRATED WORKSHOP WITH LITERACY EXPLORATION OPPORTUNITIES (LEO)

Add iZones to the Balanced Literacy Diet

Through integration of iZone themes into the workshop structure, reading and writing become embedded in daily learning and ingrained in content organically. Reading and writing are placed at the forefront of all learning in the early childhood classroom. The idea is like a *cloche*, "a bell- or dome-shaped

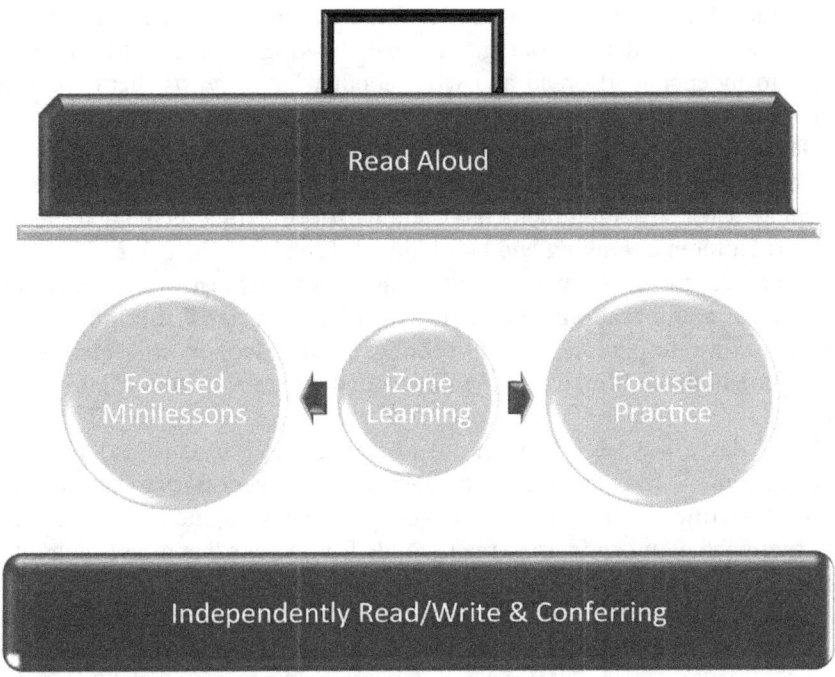

Figure 8.4 A day in the life of a reimagined literacy workshop

cover" (Merriam-Webster.com, n.d.). Figure 8.4 provides a visual of a day in the life of the workshop where iZones are at the center.

Every day is covered by a read aloud and served on independent reading and writing with conferring. Balanced and nourishing skills are served with thematic, play-based learning as the main course and minilessons and guided/independent practice as the sides. The cloche works to ensure that reading and writing unfold daily in the classroom. It protects child-centered learning and encourages balanced, systematic implicit and explicit instruction. And, it honors the importance of thematic, play-based learning.

Think Literacy Exploration Opportunities (LEO): An Integrated Workshop

Throughout this book, we have established the importance of literacy as the natural connector of skills for young children. We have introduced a new way to think about learning areas in the environment through iZones. We now propose a new way to think about reading and writing workshop.

Literacy Exploration Opportunities (LEO) is our integrated reading and writing approach that encourages critical thinking. During LEO, children begin to independently read and write about what *interests* them based on inquiry about the theme of the iZone.

Our LEO balances explicit and implicit instruction within iZones. Remember, in chapter 7, we discussed the importance of implicit and explicit literacy teaching. These teaching methods, when balanced with a theme and inquiry, support children's thinking and build knowledge.

Implementing LEO with implicit and explicit instruction will take knowledge about reading and writing development, DAP, and play. It will also take time to plan LEO within iZones to best support children's learning. Once in place, though, you will notice children's sustained knowledge flourish.

Every day always begins with a read aloud. Why? It really is simple. "If young children are going to develop the motivation necessary to sustain them through the often difficult early stages of reading development, they will need to experience many and varied read-alouds from books that are of high interest to them" (Reutzel & Cooter, 2019, p. 115).

These read alouds should be engaging, meaning that the teacher reads and *engages* the students in thinking about the text (just as was discussed in principle 5). The read aloud will be linked to the theme of the iZones and may or may not be the same one that you use for your minilessons. The choice that you make about whether to keep the same book for the read aloud and minilessons is dependent on interest, complexity of the skill or the text, and what is individually needed by children.

For example, your read aloud might model meaning-based skills, like questioning, connecting, inferring, synthesizing, vocabulary application, and reading fluency, especially prosody. You ask children to think along with you, knowing just when to interrupt the reading to promote this thinking. But, you always remember that reading aloud to the whole class at the beginning of the day serves the purpose of reading for enjoyment.

Every day, content can be built through multiple interactions with purposeful, thematic iZones (as encouraged in principle 6). These areas of play provide children opportunities to explore and inquire about themes of interest to them. They are also areas where teachers can very purposefully integrate materials and activities needed to practice specific content skills. After all, anything can be taught with literature, and integrating content is the best way for children to learn authentically.

While children are learning through inquiry in their iZones, teachers can move through the areas observing and teaching children as they play (like the examples in Principles 3 and 4). In addition, they can pull small groups for minilessons and work with individual students as they engage in independent practice. Small groups work better for minilessons than whole group instruction because you are able to differentiate for the specific students with whom you are working. You also minimize opportunities for children to get lost or distracted in their learning when they are in a large group.

For example, minilessons can include experiences where you are guiding reading. This could be a shared reading or writing experience. It could also be time for guided reading for those who are reading simple texts on an instructional level or working with the teacher on skills needed for pieces that they are writing. Just remember that if you are using a brand-new text for a minilesson, most of the time you should read it aloud to the small group first. All of this is linked thematically to the iZone. Remember how the teachers were discussing how to do this in figure 8.1? That is how this model differs from the traditional workshop; all learning can be linked, even Guided Reading (Fountas & Pinnell, 2017).

Focused practice is independent or partner practice with targeted skills. Use this time to confer with individual children and explicitly instruct where necessary. During this time, children begin to apply what they learned in the minilesson to new situations. They assimilate information and make accommodations to their existing schema. Observe and facilitate when needed. What you give children for independent practice should be extending learning through their inquiry and purposeful play in the iZone.

It is important to remember that the minilessons and focused practice should not take any one child away from inquiry-based play for too long. You have to plan this very carefully. All children deserve time for purposeful play; consider meeting the children where they are in the iZone if needed. Remember, you can provide some very solid individualized practice and instruction right there in the iZone instead of pulling them somewhere else.

A day in the life comes full circle with independent reading and writing. But, that is not the only place where independent reading and writing can occur; it is just that these are non-negotiables for us, so our cloche model gives it a spot of its own. Independent reading and writing time is a place for interest-based exposure to lots of books and writing experiences. It may or may not be related to the theme. But, you will certainly enjoy the time that you have to confer with individual students as they read and write. Don't forget that you are an integral part of the independent reading and writing time.

As you can see, a day in the life of a literacy learner is full in a thematically based literacy workshop. You are a vital component in facilitating learning in read alouds, iZones, minilessons, and focused practice sessions and conferring that work together naturally to support children through integrated reading and writing.

Go for It: Start a LEO-led Classroom

Imagine a classroom where children express an interest in learning more about jungles. The jungle theme is visible throughout. Today, you choose to start by reading aloud *Weslandia* by Paul Fleischman. Notice how flexible theme integration can be. *Weslandia* is not about an African or Rainforest jungle, but it is about a boy who creates his own jungle in his yard. The books that you choose for your workshop will be similar to the theme but do not have to be narrow.

Remember, you are reading aloud with all of the children to promote enjoyment of the text and also engage them in thinking about the text. Because *Weslandia* is a "thinking book" with higher-level vocabulary, for kindergarten children, you may want to divide the book to read over a few days. For this read aloud, we could read about half, up to the point where Wesley lets his *friends* enter *Weslandia*.

Use prosody when reading, remembering to fluctuate the tone of your voice depending on what is happening in the text. This will be essential for retaining the attention of kindergarten students. Know which vocabulary words you will stop to talk about and which ones you will not because this book is full of rich vocabulary. We don't want you to deprive young readers of rich texts simply because they are a bit challenging; you just have to adjust what you do with the read aloud.

For example, you might ask, "What does bedlam mean?" You can show them how a reader might determine the meaning. You can also ask them why Wesley's plants are growing so tall and why he has never tasted any of the fruit flavors. The children might engage in a discussion about imagination and pretend. Continue to choose ideal, and developmentally appropriate, places where children can interact with you and the text while you are reading. When you end this read aloud in the middle of the text, they will want you to read the rest the next day to find out what happens to Wesley.

After the read aloud, children move into the iZones. Your class is filled with iZones related to this theme. One example is the Jungle Books iZone.

As you are observing the children at play, you stop to watch five children in the Jungle Books iZone. In that iZone there are many books for them to look at, pretend read, or make attempts at independent reading. There are leveled books like *Who Is the Beast?* by Keith Baker; fiction books like *Where the Wild Things Are* by Maurice Sendak; or *Rain, Rain, Rain Forest* by Brenda Z. Guiberson; and nonfiction books like *Big World, Small World* from Scholastic's Planet Earth series. There are opportunities to read with friends or even stuffed animals, to record their own reading on iPads, and to draw and write about what they are reading and learning about jungles.

As you move on to observe other children, you stop at the Jungle Art iZone. There are several books to look at that might promote different types of art: *The Great Kapok Tree* by Lynne Cherry, *Just a Dream* by Chris Van Allsburg, *Rumble in the Jungle* by Giles Andreae, and *Me Jane* by Patrick McDonell. These books have wonderful illustrations and are full of information for the children to utilize in creating their art.

You notice a few children working on their art in this iZone; they previously struggled with the phonological awareness assessment. This is a perfect time to teach your planned minilesson that concentrates on rhyme. You pick up *Rumble in the Jungle* for a shared reading minilesson with them.

Since you read *Rumble in the Jungle* last week to the whole class, you can begin the minilesson by talking about rhyme, reviewing the book, and discussing how to determine rhyming words. Read the book again to focus the practice on particular rhymes and encourage children to identify words that rhyme on each page. For example, children may notice that *paws* and *jaws* rhyme. Help the children notice other words that rhyme as well. They can cover rhyming words with colored tabs or highlighter tape (using different colors on each pair of rhyming words). They can also help you write lists of rhyming words from the book too.

After the minilesson, this small group of children is ready to begin a focused independent practice in this iZone. They choose their favorite animal from the book and create that animal using an art technique known as torn paper and pasting (tearing paper to create the animal instead of using scissors). While they are working on their art, this is the perfect time for you to visit other children for whom you have planned purposeful minilessons. If possible, you can conduct your minilesson where the children are in their playful learning.

Check back later with the children in the Jungle Art iZone and guide them further in focused practice. Encourage the children to add a rhyme about their created animal. Talk with children about their animals and question them about things that rhyme with that animal or with that animal's characteristics. For example, Happy Hippo likes to flippo. Which might look something like this for the child, "Hape Hpo liks tu flpo." The child's writing can be glued either on the front or back of their torn paper animal. Let it be the child's choice.

You continue this pattern of purposeful interaction with the children as they work in iZones. You are conducting minilessons and engaging them in focused independent practice, going to them instead of having them come to you. The lessons and practice can all be connected to the inquiry-based learning that is taking place.

The last part of the workshop is independent reading and writing. Children are reading and writing based on choice, and you are conferring with them.

You might notice one of the children you worked with earlier going back to *Rumble in the Jungle*. You observe the child reading the book and hear her mimicking your earlier reading. When the story is over, the child pulls out paper and begins to write the names of the animals she remembers from the story. For example, the child is struggling while writing the word crocodile. You slide in to confer with her about the different sounds that *C* can make.

After the conference the child chooses her approximation of the spelling of crocodile with a *C* instead of a *K*. She even goes back to the text to see if she is right. This is independent practice at its finest. The child is motivated to write on her own and chooses to write about the animals that are important to her, and you have the prime opportunity to do very explicit teaching. As the rest of your children read and write, you can individualize teaching for them too.

Notice how both implicit and explicit instruction are accomplished through this integrated workshop approach. Think about the differences between LEO and a traditional reading and writing workshop. How does LEO offer children an authentic connection between skills and learning in a purposeful play setting?

Teaching through a LEO approach requires you to basically be on your toes at all times. You have to know the individual needs of your children, engage in preplanning, and be able to predict what they might say and do when you are teaching those skills. You have to understand purposeful play, DAP, and have knowledge of the skills that need to be taught.

This chapter might feel like a lot of information, and you may be thinking that you will never figure it all out. So, we have one, final word of caution that might help.

⚠ Avoid thinking, "I Can't!"

We are here to say everything that you have learned in this book is absolutely doable! Take small steps. Implement one thing at a time. Get to know your children first. If you work with your children individually and confer with them in small groups or in *alongside* reading and writing, you will be able make predictions about literacy behaviors. You *will* grow and develop into a master literacy teacher! This growing and developing takes time. The main thing to remember is that *anyone* can do this!

Appendix A: Children's Texts List

Principle 1

Because of Winn-Dixie by Kate DiCamillo
Brown Girl Dreaming by Jacqueline Woodson
Charlotte's Web by E. B. White
Finding Winnie: The True Story of the World's Most Famous Bear by Lindsay Mattick
Harry Potter series by J. K. Rowling
Holes by Louis Sachar
Island of the Blue Dolphins by Scott O'Dell
My Louisiana Sky by Kimberly Willis Holt
Out of My Mind by Sharon Draper
Thank You, Mr. Falker by Patricia Polacco
The One and Only Ivan by Katherine Applegate
Wonder by R. J. Palacio

Principle 2

A Splash of Red: The Life and Art of Horace Pippin by Jen Bryant
Christmas in Camelot Mary Pope Osborne
Giant Squid by Candace Fleming
Last Stop on Market Street by Matt de la Peña
Magic Tree House Mary Pope Osborne
Mr. Brown Can Moo, Can You? by Dr. Seuss
Spiderwick Chronicles series by Tony DiTerlizzi
Stuart Little by E. B. White
Time for Kids

The Kissing Hand by Audrey Penn

Whoosh! Lonnie Johnson's Super-soaking Stream of Inventions by Chris Barton

Principle 3

Ada Twist, Scientist by Andrea Beaty

Jack and Jill by unknown author. In A. Mills (Ed.), *The Random House Children's Treasury: Fairy Tales, Nursery Rhymes, & Nonsense Verse*

"Me I Am" by Jack Prelutsky. In J. Prelutsky & A. Lobel (Eds.), *The Random House Book of Poetry for Children: A Treasury of 572 Poems for Today's Child*

Principle 4

Catalina Magdalena Hoopensteiner Wallendiner Hogan Logan Bogan Was Her Name by Tedd Arnold

Principle 5

Barnyard Dance by Sandra Boynton
Bear Snores On by Karma Wilson
Big Fat Hen by Keith Baker
Big Red Barn by Margaret Wise Brown
Chicka Chicka Boom Boom by Bill Martin Jr.
City Dog, Country Frog Mo Willems
Click Clack Moo: Cows That Type by Doreen Cronin
David Gets in Trouble by David Shannon
Don't Let the Pigeon Stay up Late by Mo Willems
Dragons Love Tacos by Adam Rubin
Froggy's Sleepover by Jonathan London
Fireboat: The Heroic Adventures of the John J. Harvey by Maira Kalman
Five Little Monkeys Jumping on the Bed by Eileen Christelow
Flotsam by David Wiesner
From Head to Toe by Eric Carle
Goodnight Moon by Margaret Wise Brown
Hickory Dickory Dock by Keith Baker
How Do Dinosaurs Get Well Soon? by Jane Yolen and Mark Teague
How Much Is that Doggie in the Window? by Iza Trapani
If You Give a Dog a Donut by Laura Numeroff
If You Give a Pig a Pancake by Laura Numeroff

Junkyard Wonders by Patricia Polacco
Just Go to Bed by Mercer Mayer
Kitten's First Full Moon by Kevin Henkes
Knuffle Bunny by Mo Willems
Lilly's Purple Plastic Purse by Kevin Henkes
Love by Matt de la Peña
My Name Is Georgia by Jeanette Winter
No Two Alike by Keith Baker
Pat the Bunny by Dorothy Kunhardt
Pete the Cat: I Love My White Shoes by Eric Lipwin
Pig the Pug by Aaron Blabey
Polar Bear, Polar Bear, What Do You Hear? by Bill Martin Jr.
Quick as a Cricket by Audrey Wood
Ramona Quimby series by Beverly Cleary
Some Writer! The Story of E.B. White by Melissa Sweet
Ten Little Fingers and Ten Little Toes by Mem Fox
The ABC Book by Dr. Seuss
The Foot Book by Dr. Seuss
The Itsy Bitsy Spider by Iza Trapani
The Little Mouse, The Red Ripe Strawberry, and The Big Hungry Bear by Don and Audrey Wood
The Mangrove Tree: Planting Trees to Feed Families by Susan L. Roth and Cindy Trumbore
The Napping House by Audrey Wood
The Poppy Lady: Moina Belle Michael and Her Tribute to Veterans by Barbara Elizabeth Walsh
The Runaway Bunny by Margaret Wise Brown
The Three Pigs by David Wiesner
The Very Quiet Cricket by Eric Carle
The Wide-Mouthed Frog by Keith Faulkner
Twinkle, Twinkle, Little Star by Iza Trapani
Waiting by Kevin Henkes

Principle 6

Animals Nobody Loves by Seymour Simon
A Sunflower's Life Cycle by Mary R. Dunn
Balloons over Broadway: The True Story of the Puppeteer of Macy's Parade by Melissa Sweet
Froggy series by Jonathan London
Hansel and Gretel by Will Moses

In the Small, Small Pond by Denise Fleming
Ivan, the Remarkable True Story of the Shopping Mall Gorilla by Katherine Applegate
Joseph Had a Little Overcoat by Simms Taback
Life in the Pond by Craig Hammersmith
Mr. Ferris and His Wheel by Kathyrn Gibbs Davis
Pink Is for Blobfish: Discovering the World's Perfectly Pink Animals (The World of Weird Animals) by Jess Keating
Sunflower House by Eve Bunting
The Blue Whale by Jenni Desmond
The Hole Story of the Doughnut by Pat Miller
The Most Magnificent Thing by Ashely Spires
The Three Little Pigs by James Marshall
The Storm Whale by Benji Davies
The Very Hungry Caterpillar by Eric Carle
Trombone Shorty by Troy "Trombone Shorty" Andrews
Tuesday by David Wiesner
Turtle Splash! Countdown at the Pond by Cathryn Falwell
van Gogh and the Sunflowers by Laurence Anholt

Principle 7

Because by Mo Willems
Chrysanthemum by Kevin Henkes
Don't Let the Pigeon Drive the Bus by Mo Willems
Giraffe's Can't Dance by Giles Andreae
Miss Spider's Tea Party by David Kirk
Over in the Meadow by Jill McDonald
Sheep in a Jeep by Nancy Shaw
Silly Sally by Audrey Wood
The Word Collector by Peter Reynolds
Willoughby Wallaby Woo by Dennis Lee

Principle 8

Big World, Small World from Scholastic's Planet Earth series
Just a Dream by Chris Van Allsburg
Me . . . Jane by Patrick McDonnell
The Great Kapok Tree by Lynne Cherry
Rain, Rain, Rain Forest by Brenda Z. Guiberson
Rumble in the Jungle by Giles Andreae

Weslandia by Paul Fleischman
Where the Wild Things Are by Maurice Sendak
Who Is the Beast? by Keith Baker

Additional Young Adult and Adult Literature Mentioned throughout the Book

Between Shades of Gray by Ruth Sepetys
Challenger Deep by Neal Shusterman
Crazy Rich Asians by Kevin Kwan
Divergent series by Veronica Roth
Genesis by Brendan Reichs
Heartless by Marissa Meyer
Nemesis by Brendan Reichs
Sharp Objects by Gillian Flynn
The Book Thief by Markus Zusak
The Woman in Cabin 10 by Ruth Ware
To Kill a Mockingbird by Harper Lee
Twilight series by Stephanie Meyer
Unwind series by Neal Shusterman
Where the Crawdads Sing by Delia Owens

Appendix B: Resources List

Principle 1

The Children's Book Podcast (https://lgbpodcast.libsyn.com/)
All the Wonders website (www.allthewonders.com)
A Writer's Notebook: Unlocking the Writer Within You book by Ralph Fletcher
Caldecott Winners (1938–present) on the American Library Association website (http://www.ala.org/alsc/awardsgrants/bookmedia/caldecottmedal/caldecottmedal_)
Colby Sharp on Twitter (@colbysharp)
Donalyn Miller on Twitter (@donalynbooks)
Matthew Winner on Twitter (@MatthewWinner)
National Writing Project (https://www.nwp.org/)
Newbery Winners (1922–present) on the American Library Association (http://www.ala.org/alsc/awardsgrants/bookmedia/newberymedal/newberymedal)
Nerdy Book Club blog (https://nerdybookclub.wordpress.com/)
Travis Jonker on Twitter (@100scopenotes)
The Nerdy Bookcast podcast (https://podcasts.apple.com/us/podcast/the-nerdy-bookcast/id1152602297)
The Yarn podcast (https://podcasts.apple.com/us/podcast/the-yarn/id1028877816)

Principle 2

Amazon website (amazon.com)
Book Love Foundation Classroom Library (booklovefoundation.org/apply)

Booksource Classroom (https://classroom.booksource.com/classroom/ScannerApps.aspx)
Classroom Checkout (https://apps.apple.com/us/app/classroom-checkout/id837087913)
Cooperative Children's Book Center (http://ccbc.education.wisc.edu/books/detailListBooks.asp?idBookLists=42)
DOGO News for Kids (https://www.dogonews.com/)
Dolly Gray Children's Literature Award (dollygrayaward.com/)
eBay (ebay.com)
Goodwill (https://www.goodwill.org/)
Half Price Books (https://hpb.com/home?gclid=Cj0KCQjwz8bsBRC6ARIsAEyNnvpc4MSa-2T6AfMKNBeYxnovbHWB4S-74d1dTfXsaTmvGYfNBhGqLSwaAkKpEALw_wcB#product-panel-home)
International Book Project (https://www.intlbookproject.org/home/our-work/get-books-2/)
Junior Library Guild Book (https://www.juniorlibraryguild.com/grants/)
Kids Need to Read (http://community.kidsneedtoread.org/)
Lulu book publishing (www.lulu.com)
National Education Association Student Achievement (http://www.nea.org/grants)
National Home Library Foundation (http://homelibraryfoundation.org/)
NCTE Children's Book Award (https://www2.ncte.org/blog/2018/11/2019-book-awards/)
NEA Foundation Education (https://www.neafoundation.org/for-educators/student-achievement-grants/)
Newsela website (https://newsela.com/)
Notable Books for a Global Society (clrsig.org/notable-books-for-a-global-society-nbgs.html)
Notable Children's Books by the Association for Library Service to Children (http://www.ala.org/alsc/awardsgrants/notalists/ncb)
Once upon a World Children's Book Award (http://www.wiesenthal.com/about/library-and-archives/once-upon-a-world-childrens-book-award.html)
Orbis Pictus Award (https://www2.ncte.org/awards/orbis-pictus-award-nonfiction-for-children/)
Scholastic Book Club (https://clubs.scholastic.com/)
Scholastic Book Fair (http://www.scholastic.com/bookfairs/)
Scholastic Literacy (https://www.scholastic.com/teachers/articles/teaching-content/teachers-get-grant/)
Scholastic News (https://scholasticnews.scholastic.com/)
Scholastic Warehouse Sales (https://bookfairs.scholastic.com/bookfairs/events/warehouse-sales.html)

The Snapdragon Book Foundation (https://snapdragonbookfoundation.org/)
Thriftbooks (thriftbooks.com)
Time for Kids (https://www.timeforkids.com/)

Principle 3

Evidence for Learning (https://www.evidenceforlearning.net/)
iAuditor (https://safetyculture.com/)
Kaymbu (kaymbu.com)
Learning Genie (https://www.learning-genie.com/)
Microsoft OneNote
Microsoft Stickies

Principle 4

Farmer's Almanac reference book (https://www.farmersalmanac.com/)

Principle 5

Chris Van Allsburg author (https://www.hmhbooks.com/chrisvanallsburg/)
Patricia Polacco author (http://www.patriciapolacco.com/)

Principle 6

Britannica Kids (https://kids.britannica.com)
Florida Museum of Natural History's International Shark Attack File (https://www.floridamuseum.ufl.edu/shark-attacks/factors/species-implicated/)
"Hurricane Season" song by Troy "Trombone Shorty" Andrews
Math Reads (https://store.mathsolutions.com/math-reads-from-marilyn-burns-grade-1-829.html)
National Science Teaching Association (https://www.nsta.org/publications/ostb/)
Orbus Pictus (http://www2.ncte.org/awards/orbis-pictus-award-nonfiction-for-children/)
Reading Nonfiction Notice & Note: Stances, Signposts, and Strategies book by Kylene Beers and Robert Probst
Reading Rockets (https://www.readingrockets.org/books/booksbytheme)
Scholastic's "Great Picture Books to Teach Social Studies . . ." (https://www.scholastic.com/teachers/articles/teaching-content/great-picture-books-teach-social-studies-grade-k-3/)
Scholastic's "Ready-to-Go Book Lists for Teachers" (https://www.scholastic.com/teachers/collections/2017/ready-go-book-lists-teachers/)

Science News for Students (www.sciencenewsforstudents.org)
"U.S. History: Jazz" article (https://www.ducksters.com/history/us_1900s/jazz.php)
Gill (n.d.) "What Teachers Need to Know about the 'New' Nonfiction" article (https://www.readingrockets.org/article/what-teachers-need-know-about-new-nonfiction)

Principle 7

An Observation Survey of Early Literacy Achievement book by Marie Clay
"A Test for Assessing Phonemic Awareness in Young Children" article by Hallie Kay Yopp
Ekwall/Shanker Reading Inventory book by James L. Shanker and Ward A. Cockrum
Flynt/Cooter Comprehensive Reading Inventory-2 Assessment of K-12 Reading Skills in English & Spanish book by Robert B. Cooter, Jr., E. Sutton Flynt, and Kathleen Spencer Cooter
What Works Clearinghouse (WWC) https://ies.ed.gov/ncee/wwc/
Words Their Way: Word Study for Phonics, Vocabulary, and Spelling Instruction book by Donald R. Bear, Marcia Invernizzi, Shane Templeton, and Francine Johnston
"Yopp SingerTest of Phoneme Segmentation. A Test for Assessing Phonemic Awareness in Young Children article by Hallie Kay Yopp."

Principle 8

Fountas and Pinnell Leveled Book website (https://www.fandpleveledbooks.com/)
"Overview of a Day's Reading or Writing Workshop resource on website (http://www.unitsofstudy.com/resourcecenter/resource?id=560)
Scholastic Book Wizard Mobile app (https://www.scholastic.com/bookwizardmobile/)
Scholastic Book Club website (https://clubs.scholastic.com/home)

References

Adams, M. J. (1990). *Beginning to read: Thinking and learning about print* (1st MIT Press pbk. ed.). Cambridge, MA: MIT Press.

Almy, M. (1949). *Children's experiences prior to first grade and success in beginning reading*. New York: Bureau of Publications, Teachers College, Columbia University.

American Academy of Pediatrics. (2014). Literacy promotion: An essential component of primary care pediatric practice. *Pediatrics, 134*(2), 404–409. doi:10.1542/peds.2014-1384

Anderson, R. C., Wilson, P. T., & Fielding, L. D. G. (1988). Growth in reading and how children spend their time outside of school. *Reading Research Quarterly, 23*(3), 285–303.

Applebee, A. N., & Langer, J. A. (2011). A snapshot of writing instruction in middle schools and high schools. *English Journal, 106*(6), 14–27.

Atwell, N. (1987). *In the middle: Writing, reading, and learning with adolescents*. Portsmouth, NH: Heinemann.

Baumer, S., Ferholt, B., & Lecusay, R. (2005). Promoting narrative competence through adult-child joint pretense: Lessons from the Scandinavian educational practice of playworld. *Cognitive Development, 20*, 576–590. doi:10.1016/j.cogdev.2005.08.003

Bear, D. R., Invernizzi, M., Templeton, S., & Johnston, F. (2016). *Words their way: Word study for phonics, vocabulary, and spelling instruction* (6th ed.). Boston: Pearson.

Beers, K., & Probst, R. (2016). *Reading nonfiction notice & note: Stances, signposts, and strategies*. Portsmouth, NH: Heinemann.

Bridges, L. (2018, April 26). All children deserve access to authentic texts [Web log post]. Retrieved from http://edublog.scholastic.com/post/all-children-deserve-access-authentic-text

Brown, C. P., Smith Feger, B., & Mowry, B. (2015). Helping others understand academic rigor in teachers' developmentally appropriate practices. *Young Children*, *70*(4), 62–69.

Calkins, L., & Ehrenworth, M. (2016). Growing extraordinary writers: Leadership decisions to raise the level of writing across a school and a district. *The Reading Teacher*, *70*(1), 7–18.

Calkins, L., & Teachers College Reading and Writing Project (TCWRP). (n.d.). Overview of a day's reading or writing workshop. Retrieved from http://www.unitsofstudy.com/resourcecenter/resource?id=560

Calkins, L. M. (1994). *The art of teaching writing*. Portsmouth, NH: Heinemann.

Cassady, J. C., & Smith, L. L. (2004). Acquisition of blending skills: Comparisons among body-coda, onset-rime, and phoneme blending tasks. *Reading Psychology*, *25*, 261–272. doi: 10.1080/02702710490512307

Cassano, C. M. (2018). Recognizing alphabet learning and instruction. In Christina M. Cassano & Susan M. Dougherty (Eds.), *Pivotal research in early literacy: Foundational studies and current practices*. New York: Guilford Press.

Catapano, S., Fleming, K., & Elias, M. (2009). Building an effective classroom library. *Journal of Language and Literacy Education* [Online], *5*(1), 59–73.

Cavanaugh, D. M., Clemence, K. J., Teale, M. M., Rule, A. C., & Montgomery, S. E. (2017). Kindergarten scores, storytelling, executive function, and motivation improved through literacy-rich guided play. *Early Childhood Education Journal*, *45*(6), 831–843.

Children's Book Council (1995). *Choosing a child's book* (pamphlet). New York: CBC.

Christenson, L. A. (2016). Class Interactive Reading Aloud (CIRA): A holistic lens on interactive reading aloud sessions in kindergarten. *Educational Research and Reviews*, *11*(23), 2138–2145. Retrieved from https://login.proxy.tamuc.edu/login?url=http://search.ebscohost.com/login.aspx?direct=true&db=eric&AN=EJ1123082&site=ehost-live

Clay, M. M. (2005). *An observation survey of early literacy achievement* (3rd ed.). Portsmouth, NH: Heinemann.

Cloche. (n.d.). In *Merriam-Webster's online dictionary*. Retrieved from https://www.merriam-webster.com/dictionary/cloche

Collins, M. F. (2018). Storybook reading: Insights and hindsights. In Christina M. Cassano & Susan M. Dougherty (eds.), *Pivotal research in early literacy: Foundational studies and current practices* (pp. 201–237). New York: Guilford Press.

Connor, C. M., Morrison, F. J., Schatschneider, C., Underwood, P., & Crowe, E. (2009, March). *Individualizing student literacy instruction: Implications of child characteristics by instruction interactions on students' reading skill growth*. Paper presented at the Society for Research on Educational Effectiveness (SREE) Conference, Virginia.

Cooter, R. B., Jr., Flynt, E. S. & Cooter, K. S. (2014). *Flynt/Cooter comprehensive reading inventory-2 assessment for K-12 reading skills in English & Spanish* (2nd ed.). New Jersey: Pearson.

Copple, C., & Bredekamp, S. (2009). *Developmentally appropriate practice in early childhood program: Serving children from birth through age 8*. Washington, D.C.: National Association for the Education of Young Children.

Cremin, T., & Oliver, L. (2017). Teachers as writers: A systematic review. *Research Papers in Education*, *32*(3), 269–295. doi: 10.1080/02671522.2016.1187664

Crisp, T., Kenezek, S. M., Quinn, M., Bingham, G. E., Girardeau, K., & Starks, F. (2016). What's on our bookshelves? The diversity of children's literature in early childhood classroom libraries. *Journal of Children's Literature*, *42*(2), 29–42.

Daniels, H. (2002). *Literature circles: Voice and choice in book clubs & reading groups* (2nd ed.). Portland, ME: Stenhouse.

Dickinson, D. K., & Smith, M. W. (1994). Long-term effects of preschool teachers' book readings on low-income children's vocabulary and story comprehension. *Reading Research Quarterly*, *29*(2), 104–122.

Draper, M. C., Barksdale-Ladd, M. A., & Radencich, M. C. (2000). Reading and writing habits of preservice teachers. *Reading Horizons*, *40*(3), 185–203. Retrieved from https://login.proxy.tamuc.edu/login?url=http://search.ebscohost.com/login.aspx?direct=true&db=eric&AN=EJ607849&site=ehost-live

Ellefson, M. R., Treiman, R., & Kessler, B. (2009). Learning to label letters by sounds or names: A comparison of England and the United States. *Journal of Experimental Child Psychology*, *102*, 323–341.

Ellis, R. (2009). Implicit and explicit learning, knowledge and instruction. In R. Ellis, S. Loewen, C. Elder, R. Erlam, J. Philp, & H. Reinders (Series eds.), *Implicit and explicit knowledge in second language learning, testing and teaching* (pp. 3–26). Bristol: Multilingual Matters.

Erikson, E. H. (1956). The problem of ego identity. *Journal of the American Psychoanalytic Association*, *4*(1), 56–121.

Fisher, D., & Frey, N. (2012). Closely reading in elementary schools. *The Reading Teacher*, *66*(3). doi: 10.179–188; doi: 0.1002/TRTR.01117

Fisher, D., & Frey, N. (2014). Closely reading informational texts in the primary grades. *The Reading Teacher*, *68*(3), 222–227. doi: 10.1002/trtr.1317

Fletcher, R., & Portalupi, J. (1998). *Craft lessons: Teaching writing K-8*. Portland, ME: Stenhouse.

Fountas, I. C., & Pinnell, G. S. (2017). *Guided reading: Responsive teaching across the grades* (2nd ed.). Portsmouth, NH: Heinemann.

Gardner, P. (2014). Becoming a teacher of writing: Primary student teachers reviewing their relationship with writing. *English in Education*, *48*(2), 128–148. doi: 10.1111/eie.12039

Gill, S. R. (n.d.). What teachers need to know about the "new" nonfiction. *Reading Rockets*. Retrieved from https://www.readingrockets.org/article/what-teachers-need-know-about-new-nonfiction

Goldstein, P. A., & Randolph, K. M. (2017). Word play: Promoting vocabulary in learning centers. *Young Children*, *72*(1), 66–72.

Graves, D. (1983). *Writing: Teachers and children at work*. Portsmouth: NH: Heinemann.

Graves, D. (1994). *A fresh look at writing*. Portsmouth, NH: Heinemann.

Harvey, S., &. Goudvis, A. (2017). *Strategies that work: Teaching comprehension for understanding, engagement, and building knowledge* (3rd ed.). Portland, ME: Stenhouse Publishers.

Hindin, A. (2018). Engagement, motivation, self-regulation, and literacy development in early childhood. In C. M. Cassano & S. M. Dougherty (Eds.), *Pivotal research in early literacy: Foundational studies and current practices* (pp. 160–177). New York: The Guilford Press.

Hoffman, J. L., Teale, W. H., & Yokota, J. (2015) The book matters! Choosing complex narrative texts to support literary discussion. *Young Children, 70*(4), 8–15.

Hohr, H. (2000). Dynamic aspects of fairy tales: Social and emotional competence through fairy tales. *Scandinavian Journal of Educational Research, 44*(1), 89–103.

Hughes, C. A., Morris, J. R., Therrien, W. J., & S. K. Benson. (2017). Explicit instruction: Historical and contemporary contexts. *Learning Disabilities Research & Practice, 32*(3), 140–148. doi: 10.1111/ldrp.12142

International Literacy Association (ILA). (2018). The power and promise of read-alouds and independent reading [Leadership brief]. Retrieved from https://literacyworldwide.org/docs/default-source/where-we-stand/ila-power-promise-read-alouds-independent-reading.pdf

International Reading Association (IRA). (2014). *Leisure reading: A joint position statement of the international reading association, the Canadian children's book centre, and the National Council of Teachers of English* [Position statement]. Retrieved from http://literacyworldwide.org/docs/default-source/where-we-stand/leisure-reading-position-statement.pdf

Invernizzi, M., & Buckrop, J. (2018). Recognizing alphabet learning and instruction. In Christina M. Cassano & Susan M. Doughtery (Eds.), *Pivotal research in early literacy: Foundational studies and current practices* (pp. 85–110). New York: The Guilford Press.

Jablon, J. R., Dombro, A. L., & Dichtelmiller, M. L. (2011). *The power of observation: Birth to age 8* (2nd ed.). Washington, D.C.: Teaching Strategies, Inc.

Justice, L. M., Pence, K., Bowles, R. B., & Wiggins, A. (2006). An investigation of four hypotheses concerning the order by which 4-year-old children learn the alphabet letters. *Early Childhood Research Quarterly, 21*, 374–389. doi:10.1016/j.ecresq.2006.07.010

Kalb, G. R., & van Ours, J. C. (2014). Reading to young children: A head-start in life? *SSRN Electronic Journal, 40*, 1–24. doi:10.2139/ssrn.2267795

Koralek, D. (2003). *Reading aloud with children of all ages*. Retrieved from Reading is Fundamental at https://www.rif.org/literacy-central/material/reading-aloud-children-all-ages

Korat, O., Bahar, E., & Snapir, M. (2002/2003). Sociodramatic play as opportunity for literacy development: The teacher's role. *The Reading Teacher, 56*(4), 386–393.

Krashen, S. (2004). *The power of reading: Insights from the research*. Portsmouth, NH: Heinemann.

Kuhn, K. E., Raush, C. M., McCarty, T. G., Montgomery, S. E., & Rule, A. C. (2017). Utilizing nonfiction texts to enhance reading comprehension and vocabulary in primary grades. *Early Childhood Education Journal, 45*, 285–296. doi:10.1007/s10643-015-0763-9

Larson, L. C., & Rumsey, C. (2017). Bringing stories to life: Integrating literature and math manipulatives. *The Reading Teacher, 71*(5), 589–596. doi:10.1002/trtr.1652

Ledger, S., & Merga, M. K. (2018). Reading aloud: Children's attitudes toward being read to at home and at school. *Australian Journal of Teacher Education, 43*(3),

124–139. Retrieved from https://login.proxy.tamuc.edu/login?url=http://search.ebscohost.com/login.aspx?direct=true&db=eric&AN=EJ1174201&site=ehost-live

Locke, T., Whitehead, D., & Dix, S. (2013). The impact of 'writing project' professional development on teachers' self-efficacy as writers and teachers of writing. *English in Australia, 48*(2), 55–69.

Lonigan, J., Burgess, S. R., & Anthony, J. L. (2000). Development of emergent literacy and early reading skills in preschool children: Evidence from a latent-variable longitudinal study. *Developmental Psychology, 36*(5), 596–613.

Lysaker, J. T., Wheat, J., & Benson, E. (2010). Children's spontaneous play in writer's workshop. *Journal of Early Childhood Literacy, 10*(2), 209–229. doi:10.1177/1468798410363835

Marinak, B. A., & Gambrell, L. B. (2008). Intrinsic motivation and rewards: What sustains young children's engagement with text? *Literacy Research and Instruction, 47*(1), 9–26. doi:10.1080/19388070701749546

McNelly, T. A. (2018). Selecting 'just right' electronic books for the early childhood classroom. *Kappa Delta Pi Record, 54*(1), 23–29. doi:10.1080/00228958.2018.1407172

Mesmer, H. A. E, Cunningham, J. W., & Hiebert, E. (2012). Toward a theoretical model of text complexity for the early grades: Learning from the past, anticipating the future. *Reading Research Quarterly, 47*(3), 235–258.

Meyer, K. E. (2010). Collaborative approach to reading workshop in the middle years. *The Reading Teacher, 63*(6), 501–507. doi:10.1598/RT.63.6.7

Miller, D. (2013). Reading with meaning: Teaching comprehension in the primary grades (2nd ed.). Portland, ME: Stenhouse.

Miller, D. (2009). *The book whisperer: Awakening the inner reader in every child* [Kindle e-book]. San Francisco, CA: Jossey-Bass.

Miller, D., & Sharp, C. (2018). *Game changer! Book access for all kids*. New York: Scholastic.

Morrow, L. M., & Rand, M. K. (1991). Promoting literacy during play by designing early childhood classroom environments. *The Reading Teacher, 44*(6), 396–402.

Morrow, L. M., & Schickedanz, J. A. (2006). The relationships between sociodramatic play and literacy development. In D.K. Dickinson & S.B. Neuman (Eds.), *Handbook of early literacy research* (Vol. 2) [Kindle version]. Retrieved from Amazon.com

National Association for the Education of Young Children (NAEYC), & National Association of Early Childhood Specialists in State Departments of Education (NAECS-SDE). (2003). *Early childhood curriculum, assessment, and program evaluation: Building and effective, accountable system in programs for children birth through age 8* [Joint position statement]. Retrieved from https://www.naeyc.org/sites/default/files/globally-shared/downloads/PDFs/resources/position-statements/CAPEexpand.pdf

National Association for the Education of Young Children (NAEYC). (2009). *Developmentally appropriate practice in early childhood programs serving children from birth through age 8* [Position statement]. Retrieved from http://www.naeyc.org/files/naeyc/file/positions/position20statement20Web.pdf

National Council of Teachers of English (NCTE). (2017). *Statement on classroom libraries* [Position statement]. Retrieved from http://www2.ncte.org/statement/classroom-libraries/

National Early Childhood Literacy Panel (NELP). (2008). *Developing early literacy: Report of the National Early Literacy Panel*. Jessup, MD: National Institute for Literacy.

National Institute of Child Health and Human Development (U.S.) (NICHD). (2000). *Report of the national reading panel: Teaching children to read: An evidence-based assessment of the scientific research literature on reading and its implications for reading instruction*. Washington, D.C.: National Institute of Child Health and Human Development, National Institutes of Health.

Nell, M. L., Drew, W. F., & Bush, D. E. (2013). *From play to practice: Connecting teachers play to children's learning*. Washington, D.C.: National Association for the Education of Young Children.

Neuman, S. B. (1999). Books make a difference: A study of access to literacy. *Reading Research Quarterly, 34*(3), 286–311.

Neuman, S. B. (2001). The importance of the classroom library. *Scholastic Early Childhood Today, 15*(5), 12–14. Retrieved from https://login.proxy.tamuc.edu/login?url=https://search-proquest-com.proxy.tamuc.edu/docview/217918107?accountid=7083

Neuman, S. B. (2014, October). Content-rich instruction in preschool. *Education Leadership, 72*(2), 36–40.

Neuman, S. B., & Roskos, K. (1990). Play, print, and purpose: Enriching play environments for literacy development. *The Reading Teacher, 44*(3), 214–221.

Neuman, S. B., & Roskos, K. (1997). Literacy knowledge in practice: Contexts of participation for young writers and readers. *Reading Research Quarterly, 32*(1), 10–32.

Oszakiweski, H., & Spelman, M. (2011). The reading/writing workshop: An approach to improving literacy achievement and independent literacy habits. *Illinois Reading Council Journal, 39*(2), 13–26.

Paciga, K. A., Hoffman, J. L., & Teale, W. H. (2011). The National Early Literacy Panel and preschool literacy instruction: Green lights, caution lights, and red lights. *Young Children, 66*(6), 50–57.

Pearson, P. D., & Gallagher, M. C. (1983). The instruction of reading comprehension. *Contemporary Educational Psychology, 8*(3), 317–344.

Pence Turnbull, K. L., Bowles, R. P., Skibbe, L. E., Justice, L. M., & Wiggins, A. K. (2010). Theoretical explanations for preschoolers' lowercase alphabet knowledge. *Journal of Speech, Language, and Hearing Research* (JSLHR), *53*(6), 1757–1768. doi:10.1044/1092-4388(2010/09-0093)

Pentimonti, J. M., & Justice, L. M. (2010). Teachers' use of scaffolding strategies during read alouds in the preschool classroom. *Early Childhood Education Journal, 37*(4), 241–248. Retrieved from https://login.proxy.tamuc.edu/login?url=http://search.ebscohost.com/login.aspx?direct=true&db=eric&AN=EJ867592&site=ehost-live

Phillips, B. M., & Piasta, S. B. (2013). Phonological awareness and alphabet knowledge: Key precursors and instructional targets to promote reading success. In T.

Shanahan & C. Lonigan (Eds.) *Early childhood literacy-the National Early Literacy Panel and beyond*. Towson, MD: Paul H. Brooks Publishing Co., Inc.

Piaget, J. (1952). *Origins of intelligence in the child* [Margaret Cook, Trans.]. New York: International Universities Press.

Piasta, S. B., Petscher, Y., & Justice, L. M. (2012). How many letters should preschoolers in public programs know? The diagnostic efficiency of various preschool letter-naming benchmarks for predicting first-grade literacy achievement. *Journal of Educational Psychology, 104*(4), 945–958. doi:10.1037/a0027757

Piasta, S. B., & Wagner, R. K. (2010). Developing early literacy skills: a meta-analysis of alphabet learning and instruction. *Reading Research Quarterly, 45*(1), 8–38. doi:dx.doi.org/10.1598/RRQ.45.1.2

Pickett, L. (2005). Potential for play in a primary literacy curriculum. *Journal of Early Childhood Teacher Education, 25*, 267–274.

Pinkham, A., Kaefer, T., & Neuman, S. B. (2014). Taxonomies support preschoolers' knowledge acquisition from storybooks. *Child Development Research*, 1–10. doi:10.1155/2014/386762

Powell-Brown, A. (2004). Can you be a teacher of literacy if you don't love to read? *Journal of Adolescent & Adult Literacy, 47*(4), 284–288.

Puddu, M., & Fanos, V. (2012). Developmental programming of auditory learning. *Journal of Pediatric and Neonatal Individualized Medicine, 1*(1), 59–66. doi:10.7363/010111

Rand, M. K., & Morrow, L. M. (2018). The impact of pivotal research on the role of play in early literacy development. In C. M. Cassano & S. M. Dougherty (Eds.), *Pivotal research in early literacy: Foundational studies and current practices* (pp. 181–200). New York: The Guilford Press.

Rasinski, T. V., Reutzel, D. R., Chard, D., & Linan-Thompson, S. (2011). Reading fluency. In M. L. Kamil, P. D. Pearson, E. B. Moje, & P. P. Afflerbach (Eds.), *Handbook of reading research* (Vol. IV, pp. 286–319). New York: Routledge.

Reutzel, D. R., & Cooter, Jr., R. B. (2019). *Teaching children to read: The teacher makes the difference* (8th ed.). New York: Pearson.

Rosenblatt, L. M. (1994). *The reader, the text, the poem: the transactional theory of literary work* (pbk. ed.). Carbondale: Southern Illinois University Press.

Roser, N. (2012). Looking, thinking, talking, reading, writing, playing . . . images. *Language Arts, 89*(6), 405–414. Retrieved from https://login.proxy.tamuc.edu/login?url=http://search.proquest.com.proxy.tamuc.edu/docview/1022626967?accountid=7083

Roskos, K. A., & Christie, J. F. (2013). Gaining ground in understanding the play-literacy relationship. *American Journal of Play, 6*(1), 82–97.

Roskos, K. A., Morrow, L. M., & Rand, M. K. (1991). Promoting literacy during play by designing early childhood classroom environments. *The Reading Teacher, 44*(6), 396–402.

Sanacore, J. (2002). Struggling literacy learners benefit from lifetime literacy efforts. *Reading Psychology, 23*(2), 67–86. doi:10.1080/027027102760351007

Sanacore, J. (2006). Nurturing lifetime readers. *Childhood Education, 83*(1), 33–37. Retrieved from https://login.proxy.tamuc.edu/login?url=http://search.proquest.com.proxy.tamuc.edu/docview/210393079?accountid=7083

Schickedanz, J. A., & Collins, M. F. (2013). *So much more than the ABCs: The early phases of reading and writing*. Washington, DC: National Association for the Education of Young Children.

Sénéchal, M., & LeFevre, J. (2002). *Parental involvement in the development of children's reading skill: A five-year longitudinal study*. Child Development, 73(2), 445–460. doi:10.1111/1467-8624.00417

Shanker, J. L., & Cockrum, W. A. (2019). *Ekwall/Shanker reading inventory* (7th ed.). New York: Pearson.

Short, K. (2011). Reading literature in elementary classrooms. In S. Wolf, K. Coats, P. Encisco, & C. Jenkins (Eds.), *Handbook of research on children's and young adult literature* (pp. 48–62). New York, NY: Routledge.

Snow, C. E., Burns, M. S., & Griffin, P. (1998). *Preventing reading difficulties in young children* (National Academy of Sciences Committee on the Prevention of Reading Difficulties in Young Children—National Research Council, Washington, DC and Commission on Behavioral and Social Sciences and Education Report ED 416 465). Washington, DC: National Academy Press. https://doi.org/10.17226/6023.

Snow, C. E., & Oh, S. S. (2011). Assessment in early literacy research. In S. B. Neuman & D. K. Dickinson (Eds.), *Handbook of early literacy research* (Vol. 3, pp. 375–395). New York: The Guilford Press.

Snow, C., & RAND Reading Study Group. (2002). *Reading for understanding: Toward an R&D program in reading comprehension*. Santa Monica, CA: Rand. doi:10.7249/mr1465oeri

Stanovich, P. J., & Stanovich, K. E. (2003). *Using research and reason in education: How teachers can use scientifically based research to make curricular and instructional decisions*. Washington, D.C.: NICHD, Department of Education and Department of Health and Human Services.

Swift, K. (1993). Try reading workshop in your classroom. *The Reading Teacher*, 46(5), 366–371.

Teale, W. H., Brown Hoffman, E., Whittingham, C. E., & Paciga, K. A. (2018). Starting them young: How the shift from reading readiness to emergent literacy has influenced preschool literacy education. In C. M. Cassano & S. M. Dougherty (Eds.), *Pivotal research in early literacy: Foundational studies and current practices* (pp. 181–200). New York: The Guilford Press.

Teale, W. H., & Sulzby, E. (1986). *Emergent literacy: Writing and reading*. Norwood, NJ: Ablex.

Trelease, J. (2013). *The read-aloud handbook* (7th ed.). New York: Penguin Books

Verenikina, I. (2008). Scaffolding and learning: its role in nurturing new learners. In P. Kell, W. Vialle, D. Konza, & G. Vogl (Eds.), *Learning and the learner: Exploring learning for new times* (pp. 161–180). University of Wollongong Australia. Retrieved from https://ro.uow.edu.au/learning/

Vukelich, C. (1994). Effects of play interventions on young children's reading of environmental print. *Early Childhood Research Quarterly*, 9, 153–170.

Vygotsky, L. S. (1978a). Interaction between learning and development. In M. Cole, V. John-Steiner, S. Scribner, & E. Souberman (Eds. & Trans.), *Mind in society: The development of higher psychological processes* (pp. 79–91). Cambridge, MA: Harvard University Press. (Original work published 1935)

Vygotsky, L. S. (1978b). The role of play in development. In M. Cole, V. John-Steiner, S. Scribner, & E. Souberman (Eds. & Trans.), *Mind in society: The development of higher psychological processes* (pp. 92–104). Cambridge, MA: Harvard University Press. (Original work published 1966)

Warton-McDonald, R. (2018). The role of word recognition in beginning reading: getting the words off the page. In C. M. Cassano & S. M. Dougherty (Eds.), *Pivotal research in early literacy: Foundational studies and current practices* (pp. 142–159). New York: The Guilford Press.

Washor, E., & C. Mojkowski (2006/2007). What do you mean by rigor? *Educational Leadership, 64*(4), 84–87.

Wilson, L. (2012). Learning to read and the preschool years. *Childhood Education, 88*(4), 270–271. Retrieved from https://login.proxy.tamuc.edu/login?url=http://search.proquest.com.proxy.tamuc.edu/docview/1492201660?accountid=7083

Worden, P. E., & Boettcher, W. (1990). Young children's acquisition of alphabet knowledge. *Journal of Reading Behavior, XXII* (3), 277–295.

Yopp, H. K. (1995). A test for assessing phonemic awareness in young children. *The Reading Teacher, 49,* 20–29.

Yopp, R. H., & Yopp, H. K. (2006). Informational texts as read-alouds at school and home. *Journal of Literacy Research, 38*(1), 37–51.

Young, T. A., Moss, B., & Cornwell, L. (2007). The classroom library: A place for nonfiction, nonfiction in its place. *Reading Horizons, 48*(1), 1–12.

Teacher Spotlight Biographies

Chapter 1: Kelsey Pierce

Kelsey Pierce is a student at Texas A&M University-Commerce. She wants to become a teacher to lead students on a successful learning journey. She feels that it is a teacher's duty to be the voice for her students. She has always wanted to be a teacher. She wants each child to walk into her classroom and know that they are loved and believe they are capable of *anything*! Kelsey can be reached at kbabylove13@gmail.com.

Chapter 1: Gabe and Anna Silveira

Gabe Silveira was born in Brazil and lives in Houston, Texas. Gabe is a fourth-grade ELAR teacher at the Mandarin Immersion Magnet School. He graduated from the University of Houston-Downtown. He is an author of *The Texas Forum of Teacher Education* and a recovering book collector. He speaks three languages and enjoys growing slim papayas and avocados. Gabe can be reached at gabriel.anna.silveira@gmail.com.

Anna Silveira is an Interventions and Assistance Teams and Referrals Committee Chairperson at Piney Point Elementary School in Houston, Texas. She has been an administrator for three years. She loves being a proud, public school educator and providing quality service to the community. She is a lifetime purveyor of puns, captain of the grammar police, and oxford comma enthusiast. Anna can be reached at gabriel.anna.silveira@gmail.com.

Chapter 2: Joni Martino

Joni Martino is a second-grade teacher in Wylie, Texas. She earned her master of science degree in Classroom Reading from Pittsburg State University in Pittsburg, Kansas. She has teaching experience in Pre-K, first grade, Title I math, and second grade. Joni serves as a district-level literacy leader and enjoys helping others learn best practices. She likes reading about reading and writing workshop models and loves collecting quality children's literature for her classroom. She can be reached at mrsmartino@gmail.com.

Chapter 3: Maria Solis

Maria Nevarez Solis is a principal of an early childhood center in Houston ISD. She has worked over thirty years in education and is passionate about doing what is best for children. She earned her master's degree from the University of St. Thomas in Educational Leadership. Prior to that she served as Director for Early Childhood Education, Early Childhood Consultant, Early Childhood Specialist, Reading Teacher Trainer, and, her most favorite role, Classroom Teacher. She can be reached at Maria.Solis2@houstonisd.org.

Chapter 4: Isabel McHan

Isabel McHan is an early childhood educator who has taught for fourteen years. She earned her bachelor's degree from the University of Houston. She participated in Rice University's Early Literacy Leadership Academy. She was the recipient of the Martel Early Childhood Educator of the Year award from the Houston Children's Museum in 2019. Her interests include advocating for play in early childhood classrooms. She can be reached at prekatplay2016@gmail.com.

Chapter 5: Ghida Hijazi

Ghida Hijazi is an elementary school literacy educator serving in a Title I public school. She is passionate about incorporating authentic literature to cultivate students' passion and love for reading. She holds a bachelor's degree in arts, with a major in education, and is currently working on her master's degree with the University of Houston. She can be reached at ghida.hijazi@gmail.com.

Chapter 6: Brandy Green and Courtney Furhken

Brandy Green is a first-grade teacher at a public Title 1 elementary school. She earned a bachelor's degree from Texas A&M University-Commerce in Interdisciplinary Studies, with an emphasis in early childhood education. She is lead mentor for her school and served as trainer for new teachers in her previous district. Brandy has fourteen years of experience teaching first grade. She is passionate about using balanced literacy instruction to create a classroom full of reading and writing opportunities. She can be reached at Brandy.Green@wylieisd.net.

Courtney Fuhrken is a first-grade teacher at a public Title 1 elementary school. She earned a bachelor's degree from Texas A&M University in Interdisciplinary Studies, with an emphasis in early childhood education. She was selected to serve on her district's literacy leader cadre and supports her fellow teachers' literacy needs. She has twelve years of experience teaching kindergarten and six years teaching first grade. She has used reader's and writer's workshop in her teaching for seventeen years. She can be reached at Courtney.Fuhrken@wylieisd.net.

Chapter 7: Shannon Mitrisin

Shannon Mitrisin is a kindergarten teacher in the Wylie Independent School District. She taught first grade for four years and is on her seventh year teaching in kindergarten. She earned her bachelor of science in education degree from the University of Oklahoma in 2009. In 2018, she received her master of education degree in Elementary Administration from Texas A&M University-Commerce. She serves on Wylie's Literacy Leader Cadre, along with other teachers from the district, to write curriculum for K-2 students. She can be reached at shannon.mitrisin@wylieisd.net.

Chapter 8: Kecia Pilant

Kecia Pilant is a public-school educator with twenty-three years of teaching experience. She is currently completing her thirteenth year of teaching first grade in Wylie, Texas. Prior to that, she taught kindergarten, second-, third-, and a fifth-/sixth-grade multi-age classroom. She earned her master's degree in Teaching at Austin College in Sherman, Texas. On her campus, she serves as a Professional Learning Community (PLC) leader. She has worked as a mentor for new teachers. She won teacher of the year for her campus in 2016. She can be reached at kvpilant@hotmail.com.

Index

Page references for figures are italicized

The ABC Book (Seuss), 77, *147*
Adams, 112, 155
Ada Twist, Scientist (Beaty), 39, 146
aliterate, 4
All the Wonders (website), 16, 151
Almy, 57, 155
alongside read aloud/reading, 20, 28, 83, 98, 144
alphabetic principle: continuum of teaching, 116–*17*, 118–19; definition of, 116; research about, 116–*17*. *See also* approaches to literacy instruction
American Academy of Pediatrics, 73, 155
American Library Association (ALA), 16
Anderson, Wilson, & Fielding, 135, 155
anecdotal checklist, 45, *46*, 47
anecdotal notes, 47, *48*
Animals Nobody Loves (Simon), 102, 147
Applebee & Langer, 135, 155
approaches to literacy instruction: bottom-up, 135, *137*; top-down, 135, *137*
assessment: formal, 40–41, *122* (*see also Flynt/Cooter Comprehensive Reading Inventory-2 Assessment for K-12 Reading Skills in English & Spanish; An Observation Survey of Early Literacy Achievement*;); informal, 41–42 (*see also* LOOK process; observation)
avoid one-size teaching: key tips, *38*; one size fits all, 37, 39, 51; relying on one test, 40–41 (*see also* tests, large-scale); using informal observation, 41–42 (*see also* assessment; observation). *See also* LOOK process

background knowledge, 84. *See also* schema
Balloons over Broadway: The True Story of the Puppeteer of Macy's Parade (Sweet), 105–6, *147*
Barnyard Dance (Boynton), 75, 146
Baumer, Ferholt, & Lecusay, 55, 59, 155
Bear, Invernizzi, Templeton, & Johnson, 1, 120, *122*, 123, 155
Bear Snores On (Wilson), 76, 146
Because (Willems), 110, 148
Because of Winn-Dixie (DiCamillo), 9, 145
Beers & Probst, 95, 155
Between Shades of Gray (Sepetys), 9
Big Fat Hen (Baker), *78*, 146

Big Red Barn (Brown), *78*, 146
Big World, Small World (Scholastic), 144, 148
The Blue Whale (Desmond), 94, 148
body, *112*, 113–14. *See also* phonological awareness
Booksource Classroom, 34, 152
The Book Thief (Zusak), *9*
Bridges, 29, 155
Britannica Kids, 89, 153
Brown Girl Dreaming (Woodson), *9,* 145
Brown, Smith Feger, & Mowry, 66, 68, 156

Caldecott Award, 16, 151
Calkins, 2, 6, 133, 156
Calkins & Ehrenworth, 134, 156
Cassady & Smith, *112*, 156
Cassano, 111–*12*, 114, 116, 156
Catalina Magdalena Hoopensteiner Wallendiner Hogan Logan Bogan Was Her Name (Arnold), 59, 61, 146
Catapano, Fleming, and Elias, 34, 97, 156
Cavanaugh, Clemence, Teale, Rule, & Montgomery, *54*, 59, 156
Challenger Deep (Shusterman), *9*
Charlotte's Web (White), *9,* 145
checklist, 44, *45*
Chicka Chicka Boom Boom, 77, 146
Chicka Chicka Boom Boom (Martin), *77*
Children's Book Council, 76
The Children's Book Podcast, 16, 151
children's texts: appeal of, 92; evaluation of, 94–96; example in read aloud, *85–87*; importance of, 92; list of, *9, 77–78*; Lulu book publishing website, 21, 152; nonfiction text features, 102–3. *See also* taxonomic texts
Christenson, 71, 156
Christmas in Camelot (Osborne), *20,* 145
Chrysanthemum (Henkes), 125, 148
City Dog, Country Frog (Willems), *85–87*, 146

Classroom Checkout, 34, 152
classroom library: acquiring books, 23–26; authentic texts, 28–29; composed of, 22–23, *26*–27; Clay, *38,* 41, 120, 122, 156
Click Clack Moo: Cows That Type (Cronin), *77,* 146
cloche, 138, 156
close reading: defined, 97–98; process, 98–100. *See also* close reading strategies; READ
close reading strategies: ask questions/discover and research, 101–2; nonfiction features, 102–3; notice words, 103; scaffolding/fill in gaps, 100. *See also* READ
coda, *112, 113*–14. *See also* phonological awareness
Collins, *73*, 75, 156
comprehension, *121*, 124–27, *137*
concepts about print, 109–11, 118
Connor, Morrison, Schatschneider, Underwood, & Crowe, 39, 156
content, 91. *See also* integration
Cooter, Flynt, & Cooter, 41, *122*, 156
Copple & Bredekamp, 57, 58, 156
core library, 20; e-books, 28; importance of, 21–22; multicultural texts, 29–30; nonfiction texts, 27–28; setting environment, 33; steps for organizing, 32; sublibraries, 21, 23; using, 34–35. *See also* discounted book sales; fiction and nonfiction book resources; grants; multicultural resources; periodical resources
Crazy Rich Asians (Kwan), 2
Cremin & Oliver, 7, 8, 157
Crisp et al., 29, 157

Daniels, 138, 157
David Gets in Trouble (Shannon), *77,* 146
decoding, decode, 112, 119–20, *121*–24. *See also* approaches to literacy instruction

developmentally appropriate practice, xvi, 53, 56–58, 140; components/evaluation of, 57; relation to literacy, 58, 75–76. *See also* rigor
Dickinson & Smith, 80, 157
discounted book sales, 24–26; public library, *24*; resale bookstores, garage sales, thrift stores, *24*, 152–53; Scholastic Book Club, *24*, 152; Scholastic book fair, *24*, 152; Scholastic warehouse sales, *24*, 152
Divergent series (Roth), *9*
Don't Let the Pigeon Drive the Bus (Willems), 110, 148
Don't Let the Pigeon Stay Up Late (Willems), *70*, 146
Dragons Love Tacos (Rubin), 76, 146
Draper, Barksdale-Ladd & Radencich, 7, 157

Ekwall/Shanker Reading Inventory, *122*, 154
Ellefson, Treiman, & Kessler, *117*, 157
Ellis, 107, 157
encode, 112
Erikson, 39, 157
explicit instruction, 107, 114–15, 118–19, 122, 126, 140, 142–44
expressive language, xv, 115–16

Farmer's Almanac, 62–63, 153
fiction and nonfiction book resources: NCTE Children's Book Awards, *30*, 152; Notable Children's Books, *30*, 152; Orbis Pictus Award, *30*, 152–53
Finding Winnie: The True Story of the World's Most Famous Bear (Mattick), *12*
Fireboat: The Heroic Adventures of the John J. Harvey (Kalman), *78*
Fisher & Frey, 97, 157
Five Little Monkeys Jumping on the Bed (Christelow), 76
Fletcher & Portalupi, 13, 157
Florida Museum of Natural History's International Shark Attack File, 102, 153
Flotsam (Weisner), *78*
fluency, *121*, 124–27, *137*, 140
Flynt/Cooter Comprehensive Reading Inventory-2 Assessment for K-12 Reading Skills in English & Spanish, 41, *122*, 154
The Foot Book (Seuss), *77*, 147
Fountas & Pinnell, 120, 138, 157
Fountas and Pinnell Leveled Book website, 132, 154
Froggy's Sleepover (London)/Froggy series, *77*, 96, 146, 147
From Head to Toe (Carle), *77*, 146

Gardner, 7, 8, 157
Genesis (Reichs), 2
Giant Squid (Fleming), *20*, 145
Gill, 95, 154
Giraffes Can't Dance (Andreae), 114, 148
Goldstein and Randolph, *121*, 157
Goodnight Moon (Brown), *78*, 146
gradual release model, 98, 133
grants, 24; Book Love Foundation, *24*, 152; International Book Project, *24*, 152; Junior Library Guild, *24*, 152; Kids Need to Read, *24*, 152; National Education Association Student Achievement, *24*, 152; NEA Foundation, *24*, 152; National Home Library Foundation, *24*, 152; Scholastic, *24*, 152; The Snapdragon Book Foundation, *24*, 153
Graves, 7, 133, 157
The Great Kapok Tree (Cherry), 144, 148
guided reading: leveled books, 132, 138, 141; linking/connecting, 141; purposeful selection, 132–33; small group, 132

Hansel and Gretel (Moses), 94, 147
Harry Potter series (Rowling), *9*, 145

Harvey & Goudvis, 124, 125, 157
Heartless (Meyer), 2
Hickory Dickory Dock (Baker), *78*, 146
Hindin, 92, 157
Hoffman, Teale, & Yokota, 76, 158
Hohr, 84, 158
Holes (Sachar), *9,* 145
The Hole Story of the Doughnut (Miller), *106*, 148
How Do Dinosaurs Get Well Soon? (Yolen & Teague), 77, 146
How Much Is that Doggie in the Window? (Trapani), 77, 146
Hughes, Morris, Therrien, & Benson, 107, 158
"*Hurricane Season*" (Andrews), 101, 153

If You Give a Dog a Donut (Numeroff), 77, 146
If You Give a Pig a Pancake (Numeroff), 77, 146
implicit instruction, 107, 115, 118–19, 140, 142–44
integration: addressing standards, 104, *105–6*; of children's texts, 92, 94, 97 (*see also* children's texts; close reading; taxonomic texts); principles of, 92; questions about, *91*; stimulate interest, 96. *See also* Math Reads; National Science Teaching Association (NSTA); National Council of Teachers of English (NCTE); Reading Rockets; Scholastic
International Literacy Association (ILA/IRA), 22, 35, 129, 158
In the Small, Small Pond (Fleming), *90*, 148
Invernizzi & Buckrop, 116–*17*, 118, 158
Island of the Blue Dolphins (O'Dell), *9,* 145
The Itsy Bitsy Spider (Trapani), *77,* 147
Ivan: The Remarkable True Story of the Shopping Mall Gorilla (Applegate), 102, 148

iZones: defined, 61; facilitation of, 65–66, 138–44; and literacy, 62; planning for, 62–65

Jablon, Dombro, & Dichtelmiller, 49, 158
"Jack and Jill" (Mills, editor), 55, 146
Jonkers, Travis, 15, 16, 151
Joseph Had a Little Overcoat (Taback), *106,* 148
Junkyard Wonders (Polacco), 76, 147
Just a Dream (Van Allsburg), 144, 148
Just Go to Bed (Mayer), 77, 147
Justice, Pence, Bowles, & Wiggins, 116–*17*, 119, 158
just right: books, 23, 69, 71, 74–76, 79, 91, 97; conversations, 79; vocabulary/words, 6, 125, *137*

Kalb & van Ours, 69, *73*, 158
The Kissing Hand (Penn), 29, 146
Kitten's First Full Moon (Henkes), 77, 147
Knuffle Bunny (Willems), 77, 147
Koralek, 76, 158
Korat, Bahar, & Snapir, 53, 158
Krashen, 134, 158
Kuhn, Raush, McCarty, Montgomery, & Rule, 27, 158

Larson & Rumsey, 91, 92, 158
Last Stop on Market Street (de la Peña), 29, 145
Ledger & Merga, 71, *73*, 80, 83, 158
LEO, 140–44
Life in the Pond (Hammersmith), *90*, 148
Lilly's Purple Plastic Purse (Henkes), 77, 147
The Little Mouse, The Red Ripe Strawberry, and The Big Hungry Bear (Wood), 77, 1471
A Little Talk About: avoiding one size fits all, *38*; children's texts in iZones, *90*; children's texts to teach

strategies, *108*; the classroom library, 20; guiding reading thematically, *132*; learning through play, *56*; reading, 2; reading aloud, *70*; writing, 3
Locke, Whitehead, & Dix, 8, 159
Lonigan, Burgess, & Anthony, 116, 159
LOOK process, 42; know its meaning, 49–50; lead exploration, 42–43; observe with purpose, 44 (*see also* anecdotal checklist; anecdotal notes; checklist); organize, 44–49
Love (de la Peña), 76, 147
Lysaker, Wheat, & Benson, 53, 159

Magic Tree House (Osborne), *20*, 28, 145
The Mangrove Tree: Planting Trees to Feed Families (Roth & Trumbore), *78*, 147
Marinak & Gambrell, 35, 159
Math Reads, 97, 153
McNelly, 28, 159
"Me I Am" (Prelutsky), 39, 146
Me . . . Jane (McDonnell), 144, 148
Mesmer, Cunningham, & Hiebert, 120, 159
Meyer, 133, 159
Miller, 133, 159
Miller, Donalyn, 10, 15, 16, 34, 151, 159
Miller & Sharp, 21, 22, 34, 159
miscue analysis, 122
Miss Spider's Teach Party (Kirk), 123, 148
Morrow & Rand, 59, 159
Morrow & Schickedanz, 65, 66, 159
The Most Magnificent Thing (Spires), *106*, 148
Mr. Brown Can Moo, Can You? (Seuss), *29*, 145
Mr. Ferris and His Wheel (Davis), *106*, 148
multicultural resources: Cooperative Children's Book Center, *30*, 152; Dolly Gray Children's Literature Award, *30*, 152; Notable Books for a Global Society, *30*, 152; Once Upon a World Children's Book Award, *30*, 152
My Louisiana Sky (Holt), *9*, 145
My Name Is Georgia (Winter), *78*, 147

NAEYC & NAECS-SDE, 51, 159
The Napping House (Wood), *77*, 147
National Association for the Education of Young Children (NAEYC), 57, 66, 127, 129, 159
National Council of Teachers of English (NCTE), 22, 26, 97, 160
National Science Teaching Association (NSTA), 97, 153
National Writing Project, 16, 151
Nell, Drew, & Bush, 68, 160
NELP, 116, 122, 125, 160
Nemesis (Reichs), 2
The Nerdy Bookcast, 15, 151
Nerdy Book Club, 15, 151
Neuman, 21, 22, 30, 92, 160
Neuman & Roskos, 53, 65, 160
Newbery Medal, 16, 151
NICHD, 116, 122, 160
No Two Alike (Baker), *78*, 147

observation, 41–50. *See also* LOOK process
An Observation Survey of Early Literacy Achievement (Clay), 41, *122*, 154
observation tools, digital: Evidence for Learning, 48, 153; iAuditor, 48, 153; Kaymbu, 48, 153; Learning Genie, 48, 153; Microsoft OneNote, 48, 153; Microsoft Stickies, 48, 153
observation tools, nondigital. *See* anecdotal checklist; anecdotal notes; checklist
The One and Only Ivan (Applegate), *12*, 145
one-sized literacy instruction/teaching, xv, xvii
onset, *113*–14. *See also* phonological awareness

oral language, 109–10, *112,* 115, 118, *137*
Oszakiweski & Spelman, 133, 160
Out of My Mind (Draper), *12,* 145
Over in the Meadow (McDonald), 114, 148

Paciga, Hoffman, & Teale, *117*, 160
Pat the Bunny (Kunhardt), 76, 147
Pearson & Gallagher, 98, 160
Pence Turnbull, Bowles, Skibbe, Justice, & Wiggins, *117*, 160
Pentimonti & Justice, 79, 160
periodical resources: DOGO News for Kids, *30*, 152; Newsela, *30*, 152; Scholastic News Magazine, *30*, 152; Time for Kids, *30,* 153
Pete the Cat: I Love My White Shoes (Lipwin), *77*, 147
Phillips & Piasta, *112*, 160
phonics. *See* decoding
phonological awareness: continuum of, *113*–14; definition of, 111–12, *113*; deletion, 115; development of, 114 (*see also* body; coda; onset; rime); insertion/substitution, 115; research about, *112*; teaching of, 115–16, 118–19. *See also* approaches to literacy instruction
Piaget, 39, 161
Piasta, Petscher, & Justice, 116, 161
Piasta & Wagner, *117*, 161
Pickett, 65, 161
Pig the Pug (Blabey), *77*, 147
Pinkham, Kaefer, & Neuman, 95, 101, 161
Pink Is for Blobfish (Keating), 103, 148
play: facilitation of, 65–66, 140; keys for success, 68; importance of, 53, *54–55*, 57, 68; in iZones, 61–65 (*see also* iZones); and rigor, 66–67; sociodramatic, 59–61; teacher directed vs. child-centered, 59. *See also* developmentally appropriate practice

Polacco, Patricia, *80*, 153
Polar Bear, Polar Bear, What Do You Hear? (Martin), *77*, 147
The Poppy Lady: Moina Belle Michael and Her Tribute to Veterans (Walsh), 76, 147
Powell-Brown, 10, 161
print awareness, *137*
Prosody, 124–26, 140, 142. *See also* fluency
Puddu & Fanos, *112*, 161

questioning, 101–2
Quick as a Cricket (Wood), *77*, 147

Rain, Rain, Rain Forest (Guiberson), 144, 148
Ramona Quimby (Cleary), 75, 147
RAN, 116–17
Rand & Morrow, 62, 65, 66, 161
Rasinski, Reutzel, Chard, & Linan-Thompson, 119, *121*, 161
READ: example of, 99; read, ask, engage, document, *98*, 98. *See also* close reading; scaffolding
read aloud example, *85–87*
read alouds: choosing books for, 74–76; a cycle for, 74; definition of, 69, 71; engaging children in, 79–80, *81*, 140; formats of, 81–83 (*see also* alongside read aloud); importance of, 71; list of favorites, 77–78; problems and solutions, 73; scaffolding of, 76, 79 (*see also* scaffolding); talk about, 83–84
readers: making meaning, 124–27; transaction with text, 124. *See also* fluency; vocabulary
reading life: becoming a teacher who reads, 5; list of favorite books, *9*; loving reading, 4–5; questions to guide thinking about reading life, 4; teachers as readers, 10
Reading Nonfiction Notice & Note: Stances, Signposts, and Strategies, 95, 154

Reading Rockets, 96, 153
receptive language, xv
Reutzel & Cooter, 39, 40, 107, 111–*12*, 116–*17*, 119–*21*, 122, 140, 161
rigor, 66–68
rime, *113*–14. See also phonological awareness
Rosenblatt, 70–71, 124, 161
Roser, 125, 161
Roskos & Christie, 59, 161
Roskos, Morrow, & Rand, *55*, 161
Rumble in the Jungle (Andreae), 144, 148
The Runaway Bunny (Brown), *78*, 147
running records, 122

Sanacore, 69, 83, 161
scaffolding, xvi, 28, 76, 79, 84, 98–103, 133. See also READ; taxonomic texts
schema, 84, 94, 100–101. See also background knowledge
Schickedanz & Collins, *117*, 162
Scholastic: Book Club website, 132, 154; Book Wizard Mobile app, 132, 154; Great Picture Books to Teach Social Studies, 96, 153; Ready-to-Go Book Lists for Teachers, 96, 153
Science News for Students, 89, 154
Sénéchal & LeFevre, *73*, 162
Shanker & Cochrum, *122*
Sharp, Colby, 15, 16, 151
Sharp Objects (Flynn), 2
Sheep in a Jeep (Shaw), 114, 148
Short, 83, 84, 162
Silly Sally (Wood), 118, 148
Snow, Burns, & Griffin, 4, 162
Snow & Oh, 40, 41, 162
Snow & RAND, *121*, 124, 162
Some Writer! The Story of E.B. White (Sweet), *78*, 147
Spelling, grammar, mechanics. See approaches to literacy instruction
Spiderwick Chronicles series (DiTerlizzi), *20*, 145
A Splash of Red: The Life and Art of Horace Pippin (Bryant & Sweet), 28, 145
Spotlight on Practice: Fuhrken, Courtney, 92, *93*; Green, Brandy, 92, *93*; Hijazi, Ghida, 71, *72, 82*; Martino, Joni, 27, *31,* 33; McHan, Isabel, 31, 59, *60, 63,* 64; Mitrisin, Shannon, 127, 128; Pierce, Kelsey, *11*; Pilant, Kecia, *136*; Silveira, Anna, 13, *14,* 15; Solis, Maria, 49, *51*
Stanovich & Stanovich, 109, 162
The Storm Whale (Davis), 94, 148
Stuart Little (White), *28,* 145
Sunflower House (Bunting), 89, 148
A Sunflower's Life Cycle (Dunn), 89, 147
Swift, 133, 162

taxonomic texts, 95–96
Teale, Brown Hoffman, Whittingham, & Paciga, 58, 162
Teale & Sulzby, 58, 162
Ten Little Fingers and Ten Little Toes (Fox), *76*, 147
tests, large-scale, 39–40
Thank You, Mr. Falker (Polacco), *12,* 145
The Three Little Pigs (Marshall), *106*, 148
The Three Pigs (Weisner), *78*, 147
Time for Kids, 28, *30*, 145
To Kill a Mockingbird (Lee), *9*
Trelease, 4, 162
Trombone Shorty (Andrews), 100–101, 148
Tuesday (Wiesner), 99–100, 148
Turtle Splash! Countdown at the Pond (Falwell), *90*, 148
Twilight series (Meyer), *9*
Twinkle, Twinkle, Little Star (Trapani), *77*, 147

Unwind series (Shusterman), *9*
"U.S. History: Jazz" (Ducketers Education Site), 101, 154

Van Allsburg, Chris, 80, 153
van Gogh and the Sunflowers (Anholt), 89, 148
Verenikina, 79, 162
The Very Hungry Caterpillar (Carle), 95, 148
The Very Quiet Cricket (Carle), 77, 147
vocabulary: in close reading, 103; instruction of, *121,* 124–27; meaning based, *137*
Vukelich, *54,* 59, 162
Vygotsky, 65, 68, 79, 162–63

Waiting (Henkes), 77, 147
Washor & Mojkowski, 53, 163
Weslandia (Fleishchman), 144, 149
Wharton-McDonald, *121,* 122, 163
What Works Clearinghouse (WWC), 129, 154
Where the Crawdads Sing (Owens), *9*
Where the Wild Things Are (Sendak), 144, 149
Who is the Beast? (Baker), 144, 149
Whoosh! Lonnie Johnson's Super-soaking Stream of Inventions (Barton), 28, 145
The Wide-Mouthed Frog (Faulkner), *78,* 147
Willoughby Wallaby Woo (Lee), 115, 148
Wilson, 110, 163
Winner, Matthew, 16, 151
The Woman in Cabin 10 (Ware), 2
Wonder (Palacio), *9,* 145
The Word Collector (Reynolds), 110, 148
Worden & Boettcher, *117,* 163

word identification. *See* approaches to literacy instruction
word recognition. *See* decoding
Words Their Way: Word Study for Phonics, Vocabulary, and Spelling Instruction, 122, 154
workshop model: balance instruction, 135; defined, 132; gradual release, 135–37, 138; integration of iZones, 138–44; literacy workshop (reading and writing), 133, 136, 138; teaching with, *134*
writer's craft, *12,* 16–17, *137*
writer's notebook, 16
A Writer's Notebook: Unlocking the Writer Within You (Fletcher), 16, 151
writing: response to oral language and CAP, 109–11; response to PA, 116; response to alphabetic principle, 119
writing life: avoid hiding from writing, 8; being a writer, 6, 127; craft in children's texts, *12;* how writers think, 2; model of, 126; questions to guide a writing life, 7–8; teacher writing attitudes, 7; tips for a teacher writer, 13, 15

The Yarn, 15, 151
Yopp, *122*
Yopp Singer Test of Phoneme Segmentation, 122, 154
Yopp & Yopp, 27, 163
Young, Moss, & Cornwell, 31, 163

zone of proximal development, 79

Author Biographies

Kim Pinkerton is an educational consultant, writer, and literacy educator with over twenty years of experience in the field. She earned a doctorate in reading and language arts from the University of Houston. She previously served as an associate professor of reading/literacy for Texas A&M University-Commerce and the University of Houston-Downtown. She taught as an elementary teacher and developmental reading and writing instructor at the community college level. She is currently teaching literacy courses for Texas A&M University-Commerce and working as a consultant for the Teaching Learning Alliance. Her primary teaching and research interests include early literacy practices, individualized literacy instruction methods, children's and young adult literature, and past and present literacy lives of teachers.

Kim lives in Dallas, Texas, and devotes her days to being a great teacher, mother, and wife. Her bookshelves are bursting at the seams and her nightstand has a steadily rotating stack of children's and young adult literature. If you ever need to talk about books or want a recommendation, give her a call! She can be reached by email (becauseofabook@gmail.com) or on Twitter (@becauseofabook).

Amelia Hewitt holds an EdD in early childhood education. She is currently an associate professor in early childhood at University of Houston-Downtown. She has more than twenty-five years of experience as a teacher. She believes that literacy is the foundation for all other learning. Her primary area of interest is in addressing the needs of the whole child through purposeful play and developmentally appropriate teaching. Research endeavors include: focusing on the effects of music and movement on socialization of young children, process-oriented art's effects on storytelling efforts of young children, the emotional and cognitive effects of collaborative partnerships between university faculty and university students, as well as team teaching practices to enhance preservice teachers' content knowledge.

Amelia is a small-town Cajun at heart but lives in the big city of Houston. She has strong family ties and enjoys traveling. She's a mom of four: two grown kids, a husband, and a dog named Moose. She is an expert with exclamation points and having the perfect quote for the perfect time! Amelia can be reached by email (hewitta@uhd.edu) or on Twitter (@ishfulplay).

www.ingramcontent.com/pod-product-compliance
Lightning Source LLC
Chambersburg PA
CBHW061833300426
44115CB00013B/2362